Art with a Mission: Objects of the Arts and Crafts Movement

Art with a Mission:
OBJECTS OF THE ARTS AND CRAFTS MOVEMENT

PATRICIA J. FIDLER
Curatorial Assistant
Department of European Art
The Nelson-Atkins Museum of Art

INTRODUCTION BY KENNETH R. TRAPP
Curator of Decorative Arts
The Oakland Museum

SPENCER MUSEUM OF ART
The University of Kansas
March 31–May 26, 1991

OCLC#
23444035

CONTENTS

FOREWORD

PATRICIA FIDLER was a graduate intern in the department of prints and drawings at the Spencer Museum of Art when she first proposed that we organize a small exhibition of works from the Arts and Crafts movement. I am not sure of the specific impetus for her proposal, but it came shortly after the museum purchased an example of William Morris wallpaper (cat no. 120). In the course of researching objects for the exhibition, she discovered significant collections in Kansas City and the surrounding region of works from the Arts and Crafts movement in all media and from several countries. This incredible wealth of ceramics, book illustrations, prints, silver, jewelry, furniture, and Tiffany lamps available locally resulted in a much larger exhibition and this accompanying catalogue. To make a coherent and focused exhibition, we decided to include works only from the United States and Great Britain.

In conjunction with the exhibition, Pat proposed that the Spencer acquire a print by an artist associated with the Arts and Crafts movement. This print, a color woodcut by William Rice titled Bert's Iris, ca. 1920, is included in the exhibition (cat. no. 119). We are enormously pleased with the result of this project in which these wonderful objects can be studied and enjoyed by the community of University of Kansas and its surrounding audiences.

Pat Fidler acknowledges the scholars, lenders, and others involved in organizing this exhibition. On behalf of the Spencer Museum of Art, I thank Phillips Petroleum Corporation, Dick Belger, William Stout, and Allen Press Inc., who have donated funds to support publication of this catalogue.

Andrea S. Norris, Director, Spencer Museum of Art

PREFACE AND ACKNOWLEDGMENTS

SIGNIFICANT SCHOLARLY ATTENTION has been accorded the Arts and Crafts movement by museums on both the East and West coasts; major exhibitions have been organized in Princeton (1974), Boston (1987), and Los Angeles (1990), with others currently in the preparatory stages. However, with the exception of two smaller-scale, rather specialized exhibitions—one organized in 1980 by the Topeka Public Library Gallery of Fine Arts to commemorate the 100th anniversary of Rookwood and the other consisting primarily of Arts and Crafts books held at the University of Kansas City, Missouri, in 1984—the public in the vicinity of the Spencer Museum of Art has not had the opportunity to view a comprehensive exhibition presenting the decorative arts of the Arts and Crafts period. Comprised of more than 120 objects of English and American origin, the exhibition *Art with a Mission: Objects of the Arts and Crafts Movement* was organized in an attempt to correct the oversight.

Although *Art with a Mission* is not intended to rival previous Arts and Crafts "blockbusters," it offers scholars and the general public the opportunity to witness the Arts and Crafts movement as it was formulated and devised in England through the efforts of William Morris and his followers in addition to its subsequent manifestations in the United States.

The exhibition and catalogue include furniture, textiles, metalwork, stained glass, ceramics, prints, books, and photographs. While some objects were from the Spencer Museum's permanent collection or borrowed from local museums and libraries, including the Nelson-Atkins Museum, the Spencer Research Library, and the Kansas City Public Library, the bulk of the show consists of objects from private collections in the area, most of which have never before been on public display. We hope that our exhibition gives deserved scholarly attention to several important local collections.

Without the generosity of numerous local collectors, this exhibition would never have reached fruition. I would like to extend my sincere appreciation to Dick Belger, Myra Morgan, Joe and Cynthia Rogers, David Stewart, William Stout, Mr. and Mrs. Bryant Upjohn, and to those who chose to remain anonymous—all of whom acted as consultants at one time or another during the preparation of this exhibition. Bill Stout, David Stewart, and Dick Belger went above and beyond to offer suggestions when the manuscript for the catalogue was in draft form. I am most grateful for their efforts. My only regret is that we could not incorporate more objects from local collections into the exhibition and catalogue; many private collections in the area still deserve recognition.

With only one year from the exhibition's conception to implementation, the staff at the Spencer Museum deserves a great deal of credit for carrying out the myriad tasks associated with the exhibition and catalogue. First and foremost, I am indebted to Dr. Andrea Norris, director of the Spencer Museum, for allowing me the opportunity to undertake this project as a curatorial intern. She allowed the idea for the exhibition to develop and grow, offering suggestions and guidance at every stage. I am grateful to Dr. Stephen Goddard, curator of prints and drawings, under whose supervision I began to organize the show and who kindly offered advice regarding the graphic art included in the show. I am also deeply indebted to Doug Tilghman, assistant director, and Barbara Becker, accounting assistant, for handling the financial details of the project; Carolyn Chinn Lewis, administrative assistant, who provided assistance with various correspondence and exhibition labels, Linda Bailey, former development coordinator, for pursuing potential avenues for funding; Janet Dreiling, registrar, and Bonnie Speed, registration intern, who conscientiously attended to the transportation and temporary storage of the objects; Jon Blumb, photographer, and Alex Fischer, photography assistant, who are responsible for the superb photographs that illustrate the catalogue; Cathy Evans, managing editor, and Ami Williams, publications assistant, for swift yet meticulous editing of the catalogue manuscript and overseeing the publicity for the show; Susan Stringer, graphic designer, for the attractive catalogue design; Bob Lowery, matter and framer, who ensured that the works on paper were ready for display; Mark Roeyer, exhibition designer, and Dan Coester, museum exhibition technician, who competently organized the installation of the exhibition; and Pat Villeneuve, curator of education, Carissa Culling, museum services coordinator, and Betsy Weaver, docent program coordinator, for devising educational activities and tours in conjunction with the exhibition.

Particularly deserving of recognition is Kenneth Trapp, curator of decorative arts at the Oakland Museum. One of the most respected scholars of the Arts and Crafts movement in the United States, Mr. Trapp kindly agreed to take time from his hectic schedule (which includes the organization of a large show on California Arts and Crafts for the Oakland Museum) to write an introductory essay for our exhibition catalogue. His introduction provides not only an interesting historical and stylistic account of the Arts and Crafts movement but also a thoughtful analysis of some areas of research that have yet to be adequately explored. I am indeed grateful to Mr. Trapp for contributing to our project. In addition, I would like to thank Marc Wilson, George McKenna, Ann Erbacher, Cindy Cart, Stacey Sherman, and Marla Cling at the Nelson-Atkins Museum and Anna E. Horn at the Kansas City Public Library, and the staff at the Spencer Research Library for their generous assistance in arranging and processing loans.

On a personal note, I would like to thank Donald Sloan for his generous support of my academic pursuits. Mr. Sloan is not only responsible for the endowed graduate internship that I held in 1989–90, he also kindly provided an additional stipend for travel and research related to the organization of the exhibition. I am also most grateful to Carol Inge and Janet Carpenter for their encouragement and advice throughout the course of this project. Finally, a special thanks goes to Victor Bailey, who offered ideas, inspiration, and support that enabled me to realize the task at hand.

Patricia J. Fidler

INTRODUCTION

Art is not simply an amusement, an indulgence which delights the fancy of the idle and rich. It is decidedly practical, and concerns the well-being, the advancement, the pleasure, of the laborer and the poor. Whenever art is applied to the simplest, commonest product of labor, there will come order, intelligence, grace, and increased value. Art is not the privilege of a class; it is essentially human, and is both individual and universal.[1]

[1]George Ward Nichols, *Art Education Applied to Industry*. (New York: Harper & Brothers, 1877), 21.

THESE IMPASSIONED WORDS by George Ward Nichols in *Art Education Applied to Industry* of 1877 were inspired by his visit to the Centennial Exhibition of 1876 in Philadelphia. Nichols, a patron and assiduous promoter of the arts in Cincinnati, was also influenced by John Ruskin and other British philosophers who expounded theories of social reform and called for the redemption of art, most particularly the applied arts, in the second half of the nineteenth century.

Nichols posited a theory of the unity of art, noting that the barriers separating the arts into hierarchies of "high," or fine, and "low," or applied, were artificial. Painting, sculpture, and architecture were considered fine arts while the traditional crafts of pottery, woodworking, textiles, glass, and metalworking were classified as applied arts. Nichols professed that these hierarchical divisions were falsely associated with cultural and moral values—the applied arts being linked with the lowest values. He felt that his mission was to persuade his fellow Americans to reunite the arts by applying art to industry. More than a theorist, Nichols suggested practical means to reunify the arts. The adoption and application of artistic principles by industry would come, he argued, through education.

He asserted that the highest aim of such application should be "to unite the useful, which is the end of industry, with the beautiful, which is the end of art."[2] Taken from Ruskin, this simple phrase succinctly encapsulates the fundamental principle of what would become the Arts and Crafts movement in its many manifestations. By writing *Art Education Applied to Industry,* Nichols added his voice to the rising chorus of advocates of social and design reform in Great Britain and the United States. His treatise was an early and important champion of design in American industry. Sped by the Centennial Exhibition, the forces that would lead to the establishment of the Arts and Crafts movement in the United States were set in motion by the 1870s. With each new voice, publication, and art industry and workshop, the foundation of the movement was laid solidly and securely.

[2]Nichols, *Art Education,* 155.

Art with a Mission, the title of this exhibition, captures the heart of the Arts and Crafts movement—to reunite art with life. The original mission of the movement was nothing short of reformation of the social structure of Great Britain and the United States to counter the adverse effects of the Industrial Revolution and restore a humane balance to life.

Although the Industrial Revolution of the late eighteenth and early nineteenth centuries created new wealth and gave rise to the middle class, it also caused much misery, laid waste to the earth, and widened the chasm between the rich and the poor. In the rush toward unbridled industrialization, manual labor was devalued, stripped of its dignity and honor. The workers became mere tenders of machines and were not to assert themselves in any creative manner. For many, the factory system and its sweatshops were, in effect, a form of slavery.

Visionaries believed that the evils of the Industrial Revolution could be mitigated by restoring the value of manual labor and reinstating the dignity and honor of the individual. The restoration of the value of manual labor, and hence of the laborer, was believed possible through individual handwork and small workshops, where traditional tools and limited industrial technology would be used by artisans. It was commonly held that work had redemptive powers, a view not vastly different from our contemporary regard for its therapeutic value.

Seeds of what would become the Arts and Crafts movement were planted in the 1850s and germinated in the 1860s and 1870s as the Art movement—or so-called Aesthetic movement championed by the aesthete Oscar Wilde—but the Arts and Crafts movement did not receive its name until 1888. That year, bookbinder T. J. Cobden Sanderson suggested the name be used for the first exhibition of the Arts & Crafts Exhibition Society in London. In 1897 the term "Arts and Crafts" was appropriated by two separate societies founded in the United States, the first in Boston and the second soon afterward in Chicago, thus giving the Arts and Crafts movement in the United States its name.

Milestones used to date the inception of the Arts and Crafts movement on the two sides of the Atlantic include the Great Exhibition—more popularly known as the Crystal Palace exhibition—in London in 1851 and the Centennial Exhibition of 1876 in Philadelphia. Each of these international expositions forced its receptive host nation to see its own art manufacturers in an unflattering light when compared to the industrial arts of rival countries. For example, the British saw theirs in contrast to the French and the Americans viewed theirs in contrast to the British. The Centennial Exhibition helped spread and popularize the ideals of John Ruskin, William Morris, and other British reformers in the United States. That world's fair, the first to be hosted by the United States, exposed Americans to the choicest art manufactures of Great Britain and France. Most important, it introduced Americans to the wares of Japan.

The theoretical foundation of what was to become the Arts and Crafts movement in Great Britain was laid by John Ruskin. His *Seven Lamps of Architecture* (1849) and *Stones of Venice* (1851–1853) eloquently idealized the medieval European cooperative relationship of artists and guild craftsmen who created the majestic Gothic cathedrals and public monuments. That relationship, he believed, provided a model that could help address the social ills arising from rampant industrialization. For Ruskin, the Gothic represented a workshop system of artistic production that was honest and sincere and instilled a sense of happiness in the lives of the workers. The Gothic gloried in decoration drawn from nature. In nature—God's book of inspiration—an endless source of decorative subjects imbued with profound meanings lay before the humble artist.

By mythologizing the medieval Gothic as the perfect model for the worker in an industrialized society to emulate, Ruskin indulged in nostalgia and created a romantic ideal—a pre-industrial arcadia—that was as distant from reality as the picture of bleakness that he often took to be the truth for his own time. As the nineteenth century lengthened and more rips seemed to appear in the social fabric than there was thread to mend them, nostalgia for the medieval grew and flourished.

If Ruskin was the numen, then William Morris was his missionary. What Ruskin declared, Morris endeavored to practice. In 1861, Morris formed the cooperative firm of Morris, Marshall, Faulkner & Co. in London to create well-designed and well-executed household furnishings. Morris's working partners were his friends—painters Edward Burne-Jones, Dante Gabriel Rossetti, and Ford Madox Brown, and architect Philip Webb. The need for such a firm was great, for the mechanization of traditional crafts that produced household wares was followed by a marked decline in artistry and quality. But to suggest that mechanization alone was responsible for this state of decline in British decorative arts is to ignore an important point. Simply put, the notion of "quality of life" as we now understand it had not yet received popular attention. That even the most ordinary and necessary household goods and utensils could be designed to contribute positively to an aesthetically harmonious quality of life in the home was not a generally recognized truism in mid-nineteenth-century England.

Although the objective of the Arts and Crafts movement in theory was to merge art and social reform, in reality, the philosophies of Arts and Crafts followers varied, making it difficult to pinpoint one unequivocal purpose for the movement. Was it a design reform movement that sought to elevate the decorative arts to the level of fine arts, paying only passing attention to social concerns? Or was it a social reform movement that used art to send its message? Even at the time of the movement, its definition varied, depending upon one's station and world views. An upper middle class woman shopping for furniture might have seen the Arts and Crafts movement as a "style" that was new and fashionable. On the other hand, a teacher in the schools of Chicago in the first decade of the twentieth century might have looked at the movement as an avenue for underpriviliged pupils—many of them recent immigrants—to find gainful work as craftspeople rather than as laborers in stockyards and factories or domestic servants and toilers in sweatshops.

To attempt precise definition of the Arts and Crafts movement, however, is to run willingly before a firing line. There are as many definitions of the movement as there are people attempting to define it. The problem is that the Arts and Crafts movement did not have a single voice, philosophy, or goal and several versions of the movement were spread over at least three continents. Within the broad sweep of the Arts and Crafts movement are artistic styles that bear their own names and identities—the Aesthetic movement; American Renaissance; the Belgian-French Art Nouveau and its Continental variations, German and Austrian-Hungarian secession; and moderne. These movements are cousins within an extended family whose progenitors gave birth to the movement in Great Britain.

Difficult as it is to define the Arts and Crafts movement, we must not be intimidated or overwhelmed by even the most modest attempt. To begin with, the movement as it evolved on both sides of the Atlantic can be defined specifically by time, place, and major supporters. What we call the Arts and Crafts movement was born in Great Britain in the mid-nineteenth century and spread across the Atlantic to the United States and Canada and as far as Australia. Even though it had tremendous influence upon design reform movements on the Continent that are known by other names, the movement was a phenomenon of the English-speaking world. It spanned the second half of the nineteenth century and the first three decades of the twentieth century. This defining period is generally accepted by scholars, although some will argue its length. If there were a time of a "pure Arts and Crafts style, however, it would cover a brief period from the mid-1890s to the First World War.

Some would argue that the Arts and Crafts movement was a system of values expressed in ideologies, not an artistic style manifested in objects. The movement is both. Whether we choose to call it such, there is a "style," "look," or "quality" that distinguished an object as Arts and Crafts. Without some accepted and agreed upon aesthetic criteria to determine what an Arts and Crafts object looks like, we would have no common language by which to understand one another when we refer to something as Arts and Crafts. The Arts and Crafts "style," however, was not codified and carved in stone.

The movement was not a monolithic phenomenon that progressed in a steady linear pattern of evolution. The early movement is often viewed, from our distance of more than a century, as nothing more than a reaction to the machine in a cause-and-effect relationship, with the movement promising redemption for the toilers in mills and factories and salvation through simple virtues of handicraft. Such an approach is of course simplistic and misleading. To be sure, there is some truth in this synopsis, but the movement encompasses a multitude of philosophies that are at times contradictory. What we know about the movement comes almost wholly from the writings of the educated and upper-middle classes. The voice of the working class remains mute, much as it always has. Its absence presents a problem, especially as it relates to issues of labor and consumption; for what was written about labor was not written by the laborer but by the capitalist, whose agenda certainly was not hidden. Only when the lives of those who performed the labor of the Arts and Crafts movement are brought into perspective will we have a clearer understanding of the movement and the degree to which it succeeded or failed.

Although the Arts and Crafts movement and its reformist principles were transplanted from Great Britain to the United States, the American movement is no mere extension of the British movement. The movement in the United States is, rather, a child of British parent—and, like any child, a unique creation. Unlike Great Britain, the United States had no aesthetic or social prophets with the commanding eloquence or charisma of John Ruskin or William Morris to provide national direction to the movement. In the United States, the movement assumed major regional variations. While there was no Gothic tradition in the United States to inspire and invigorate the movement, the youthful nation's own British colonial tradition along the Eastern seaboard and its Spanish colonial tradition in the Southwest and California offered the closest semblance of a distant European-centered past. In the Southwest and California, the Franciscan missions established a historic and regional identity.

Americans did not suffer the rigid British class system that compromised any hope of the democratization of the arts. Perhaps most revealing in the differences between the Arts and Crafts movements of Great Britain and the United States is the attitude toward the machine. That Americans were in general more accommodating of machines than the British should be no great surprise. Machines had served the North to win the Civil War; machines helped open the frontiers of the West; and machines made possible the most goods for the most people at the lowest prices, however much these goods may have been despised by arbiters of taste. So vast was the United States that relatively few people had experienced the "dark satanic mills" of machine production known to the British.

Still, from the mid-1870s to the 1930s—which encompassed the Arts and Crafts movement—social and cultural changes were so vast and dramatic in the country as to challenge even the most fertile imagination. The United States, consolidating a continent from the Atlantic to the Pacific and from the Gulf of Mexico to the Great Lakes, changed from an agricultural, rural society to an industrial, urban nation. Major industrial and manufacturing giants began to dominate. Department stores were established; the "sciences" of advertising and marketing were developed; advancements were made in lighting, communication, radio, and film; a national rail system was established; and the automobile, airplane, and modern home appliances were invented. At the same time, the women's movement was growing and an environmental movement was beginning. All of these changes had an impact on the attitude of the country and influenced the form the Arts and Crafts movement took in the United States.

As the movement spread across the country from large cities to small towns and villages, clubs, handicraft guilds, and societies sprang up to popularize the movement and to keep its tenets vital. These organizations ranged in size from several hundred members to a handful of adherents. Besides promoting the ideal and spirit of handiwork, these guilds and societies often served as exchanges for the marketing of the arts. Perhaps their most important role, however, was that of educator. Never before in the United States had the visual arts been so democratized, so enjoyed by so many people at all socio-economic levels. Indeed, the greatest success of the movement may well have been in its educational efforts.

The Arts and Crafts movement entered the American home in the form of publications directed at women, such as shelter magazines and home manuals. *Art Amateur, China Decorator, Home Decorator and Furnisher, Art Interchange, House Beautiful, Ladies' Home Journal, Keramic Studio, House and Garden,* and countless other periodicals informed women how to dress, cook, decorate their homes, and care for children. By the turn of the century, a common theme was how to live the simple life. In the early years of the twentieth century, the simple life came to represent the virtuous life.

Women were obviously targeted as important Arts and Crafts consumers, but their role in the formation and transmission of the Arts and Crafts movement has yet to receive thorough investigation. They were vital in shaping the character of the movement not only as consumers, but as producers, philanthropists, theoreticians, and critics. A few women envisioned the applied arts as avenues of honorable, meaningful, and gainful work at a time when women were severely restricted in their activities outside the home. Predictably, most women pursued arts considered appropriate for their sex—china painting, pottery decorating, decorative wood carving, and needlework—although a few attempted other crafts, such as metalwork and jewelry making.

A marked feature of the Arts and Crafts movement, one that grew out of the Victorian obsession with cataloguing and categorizing, is the plethora of published treatises on the principles of design. The notion that art and design could be reduced to codified series of "correct" principles resided in the nineteenth-century belief in scientific determinism. Anything real, it was held, could be precisely defined and quantified—even art. In general, these treatises postulated a few rules that, if followed, would lead to what was correct.

Historicism—the borrowing of designs from historical traditions—became a frequent feature in Arts and Crafts productions. As the movement matured in the United States, many artists were inspired by Native American traditions from the Great Plains and the pueblos in the Southwest. Native Americans were seen by Arts and Crafts followers and buyers as untainted and uncorrupted by an effete civilization or its industrial system. The American Indian was idealized as the noble savage who lived harmoniously in and with nature, taking no more than was needed.

The artistic tradition that exerted the most enduring influence upon design in the United States in the late nineteenth and early twentieth century was that of Japan. So widespread and far-reaching was the influence Japan would later exert on American art manufactures that only recently has that influence begun to receive the rigorous scholarly attention it deserves. Japanese art was extolled for its spontaneous brevity and its lyrical evocations, which suggested nature but did not attempt to capture it in photographic detail. The reality of Japanese art was the "correct" reality, for it captured the essence of an experience.

Naturalism in decoration was commonly disdained by the Arts and Crafts theorists as slavish copying that could never produce more than an approximation of the subject. Rather, they declared that conventionalization—abstracted stylization that did not lose its representational qualities—was the most desirable decoration. Still, nature remained the fountainhead of all that was considered vital and original in the best of designs.

Whether expressed in town planning, architecture, gardens, graphic designs, ceramics, glass, textiles, bookbindings, jewelry, or furniture, the Arts and Crafts style emphasized simple architectonic forms, subdued colors, inconspicuous finishes, and semi-precious metals and stones that all contribute equally to a synthesized design. The quintessential Arts and Crafts objects—in the popular mind at least—are Gustav Stickley or Stickley-like pieces of furniture, Will Bradley posters or magazine covers, or Grueby or Rookwood simple-shaped vases with mat glazes in solid colors. These represent the norm against against which other artistic manifestations of the Arts and Crafts movement are measured.

If there were a time of a "pure" Arts and Crafts style, it would cover a brief period from the mid-1890s to the First World War. Some scholars point to the First World War as marking the demise of the Arts and Crafts movement. Others assert that what the First World War failed to kill in the movement's vitality, the Great Depression and the Second World War finished. There is, however, a growing sense that the Arts and Crafts movement did not die with the combined calamities of two world wars and the global economic collapse between them, but that the movement simply entered an extended period of suspended animation, to awaken later with new vigor. Today many small workshops, such as those that produce glass, draw inspiration from traditional techniques while entertaining new technical and aesthetic approaches to the medium. Similar transmutations are visible in the revival of "art furniture," "art ceramics," and "art fiber." This is not to say that the contemporary craft movement is nothing more than a continuation of a once vibrant tradition. To the contrary, the contemporary craft movement has the same relationship to the Arts and Crafts movement as the butterfly has to the chrysalis.

Interest in products of the movement has reached an almost fevered pitch, as is obvious from the increase of Arts and Crafts publications, exhibitions, scholarly symposia, conferences, college courses; the astronomical rise in price that works command at auction; and the growth in a nationwide network of "pickers" and "antiquers" who scour flea markets, yard and estate sales, and classified advertisements for choice bargains. Why do objects that were, hardly more than a century ago, scorned as embarrassing examples of Victorian clutter and kitsch now excite admiration and imitation? What does this remarkable rediscovery of the Arts and Crafts movement say about how we see ourselves and our lives? At a time when art seems to be the privilege of not just the rich, but the super rich, when it seems more controversial and confrontational than uplifting, and when it is often a barrier that separates the educated from the uneducated and the "haves" from the "have nots," we look back nostalgically to an era less distracted and far more optimistic than our own.

Kenneth R. Trapp, Curator of Decorative Arts, The Oakland Museum

THE ARTS AND CRAFTS MOVEMENT IN ENGLAND AND THE UNITED STATES

CONCEIVED AS A PROTEST against damaging effects of mid-Victorian industrialization on the decorative or minor arts in England, the Arts and Crafts movement evolved by the turn of the century into a mission to preserve handicraft traditions and to ameliorate working conditions of artists and craftsmen. Reformers provided a new aesthetic standard based on simplicity and harmony to replace the ostentatious, eccentric tastes that prevailed. Although the Arts and Crafts movement did not receive its name until 1888, several British intellectual leaders formulated the philosophical argument behind the movement much earlier. In the late 1830s designer and writer August Welby Northmore Pugin (1812–52) promoted an alternative to the monotony of factory work and the decline of craftsmanship and design. Dispirited by the corruption of Victorian society, he advocated a return to the Middle Ages, perceived as a purer and more spiritual time, to restore stability to society and integrity to design. Moreover, Pugin felt that Gothic architecture, characterized by simplistic, functional designs, should be adopted as England's national style.

Like Pugin, John Ruskin (1819–1900), Oxford University's first art history professor, promoted an anti-industrialist philosophy and a return to the Gothic style, especially in architecture. In his book *Stones of Venice* (1851–53), Ruskin envisioned the satisfaction felt by medieval craftsmen who, through skill and imagination, made objects of beauty. In contrast, he believed the machine produced only lifeless, meaningless things. Ruskin strove for the reintegration of hand labor into artistic production and championed the medieval guild system. In 1871 he founded one of the period's first Arts and Crafts communities, the Guild of St. George.

As a student at Oxford, William Morris (1834–96) was well-versed in the writings of Pugin and Ruskin and did more to translate their ideas into reality than anyone before him. Eschewing mechanization and embracing medieval models, Morris founded the decorating firm of Morris, Marshall, Faulkner and Company in 1861 (after 1875 known as Morris and Company) and the Kelmscott Press in 1890. Although he was more the practitioner than Pugin or Ruskin, Morris was also concerned with the philosophical and social implications of the Arts and Crafts movement. He devoted the latter part of his career to the socialist movement, writing extensively and lecturing throughout England on the subject.

Morris's outspoken advocacy of social and political reform and his talents as a designer gained the attention of many English artists and craftsmen, who adopted and disseminated the tenets of the Arts and Crafts movement by founding guilds, societies, and art schools in the 1880s and 1890s. The most influential of these groups was the Arts and Crafts Exhibition Society founded in 1888. Within the first year of its existence, this society organized a landmark exhibition in London that consisted of more than 500 crafted objects, including furniture, metalwork, jewelry, glass, ceramics, and needlework. Each craftsman and designer was credited for his or her entry. With the overwhelming success of this exhibition, the Arts and Crafts Exhibition Society gave its name to the developing artistic movement.

From its inception, however, the Arts and Crafts movement did not represent a single, collective style. The stylistic boundaries of Morris and

Company's production, for instance, stretched from richly ornamented medieval designs to simplistic, austere vernacular works. This diversity was echoed in other English workshops. It is possible, nonetheless, to identify several unifying characteristics of Arts and Crafts objects made in England and later in the United States. The objects are functional yet aesthetically pleasing; they illustrate total attention to material and technique; and they are often ornamented with motifs derived from nature.

Although the Arts and Crafts movement originated as a revolt against industrialization, it was never entirely divorced from the factory and machine. In the beginning, Morris idealistically insisted that his firm continue the handicraft tradition and shun mechanization. As a result, Morris and Company goods, which required a great amount of hand labor, were too expensive for the average person. Labeling Morris an elitist, some English design reformers opted to use the machine—to varying degrees—to lower production costs. Arthur L. Liberty (1843–1917) became famous for his affordable line of metalwares, which were mass-produced in the Arts and Crafts style. The contradictory stance toward the utilization of the machine was also seen in the production of other mediums, including ceramics and glass. Some ceramics studios insisted on a complete separation from automation, but others employed machines to mix clays and used mass-produced molds to shape vessels.

Outside England, the Arts and Crafts movement was equally complicated and difficult to define. The United States was introduced to the movement by various intellectual figures who had met John Ruskin or studied his writings. Charles Eliot Norton (1827–1908), the first professor of fine arts at Harvard University, was a close friend of Ruskin and became the first president of the Boston Society of Arts and Crafts (founded in 1897). A professor at the University of Chicago, Oscar Lovell Triggs (1865–1930) founded the Chicago Arts and Crafts Society and wrote extensively on the Arts and Crafts movement in the Midwest.

Many other American reformers and educators promoted the Arts and Crafts philosophy, but they have been overshadowed by the movement's advocates whose enterprises proved commercially successful. Considered two of the leading proponents of the American Arts and Crafts movement, Gustav Stickley (1857–1942) and Elbert Hubbard (1865–1915) were essentially businessmen and entrepreneurs who, for the most part, removed themselves from the movement's theoretical and political issues. Stickley produced furniture, metalwork, and textiles under his Craftsman label that were useful, honestly constructed, and beautiful and sold them through major American department stores, including Sears and Roebuck. In addition, his magazine, called *The Craftsman,* which featured technological and educational articles, reviews of Arts and Crafts exhibitions, and advertisements for Craftsman objects, influenced the direction of the Arts and Crafts movement in the United States. Elbert Hubbard, a born salesman, co-owned a soap company before selling his share to open a crafts company in East Aurora, New York. Hubbard marketed his printed products from the Roycroft Press, metalwork, and furniture through a mail-order catalogue. Seeking to enlarge a market for his wares, Hubbard also produced his own magazines, called *The Philistine* and *The Fra.*

Despite their concentration on the artistic and commercial aspects of the Arts and Crafts movement, Stickley and Hubbard were aware of the movement's provenance and credo; they were familiar with Ruskin's writings and visited England in the 1890s. Yet they chose to market the Arts and Crafts style without promoting social reform. This was partly because Americans were not as violently opposed to industrialization as were the English. To combat high costs of craftsmanship, Stickley and Hubbard relied partially on the machine to produce their goods. The controversy in England over the use of mechanization did not ensue to any great degree in the United States, and the machine was more readily accepted and employed in the United States. Some American craftsmen, however, refused to use the machine and organized studios in the tradition of a studio or guild, recalling the halcyon days of the Middle Ages. In the end, these studios usually had a difficult time making a profit and were unable to stay in business unless otherwise subsidized.

The financial success of Stickley and Hubbard encouraged many other artists and craftsmen throughout the United States to adopt the tenets of the Arts and Crafts movement and apply them to various mediums. Ceramic production reached its zenith in the United States during the Arts and Crafts period with workshops in California, Colorado, Massachusetts, Missouri, New Orleans, and Ohio. The production of the graphic arts, including books, prints, and posters, was also greatly enhanced. In an age of mechanization, artists and craftsmen attempted to reintroduce simple, straightforward techniques and improve standards of printing.

The Arts and Crafts movement pervaded all aspects of English and American decorative arts, from furniture to ceramics, metalwork to glass, and books to posters. The movement, however, did not achieve all that its founding fathers set out to do. The Gothic style was not adopted as a national program for design in England or the United States, but instead diverse influences, including an emphasis on nature, led to an incredible variety of design. Moreover, significant social and political reform did not materialize in England or the United States as a consequence of the movement. Despite all the complexities and philosophical contradictions of the movement, one can safely interpret its success—the movement accorded the decorative arts a position of stature for the first time in the history of art and elevated the status of the craftsman to that of artist.

FURNITURE

MORRIS, MARSHALL, FAULKNER AND CO. (1861–75)
OR MORRIS AND CO. (1875–1940)
LONDON, ENGLAND

William Morris (1834–96) was undoubtedly the greatest creative force behind the Arts and Crafts movement. As a poet, philosopher, designer, and revolutionary socialist, Morris dedicated his life to the unification of art and labor. In a revolt against industrialized Victorian society, Morris advocated a return to handicraft methods of the Middle Ages so that pleasure could be restored in the workplace and better-quality, affordable items would be produced. His designs signified an effort to rid the world of the extravagant ornamentation and impractical, eclectic forms of high Victorian decorative arts.

As a student at Oxford University in the 1850s, Morris discovered the writings of John Ruskin (1819–1900), an influential art critic who promoted a revival of Gothic architecture. At the same time, Morris became closely associated with the Pre-Raphaelite Brotherhood, a group that sought an art as pure and spiritual as that which they believed flourished before the Renaissance. In 1859 Morris married Jane Burden, a red-haired beauty who modeled for many Pre-Raphaelite paintings, including Dante Gabriel Rossetti's *La Pia de' Tolomei* (1880), now in the collection of the Spencer Museum of Art.

Morris experimented with architecture, poetry, and painting before finding his true vocation as a furniture and pattern designer. He created medieval-style furnishings for his first home, Red House, which led to the foundation of the manufacturing and decorating firm of Morris, Marshall, Faulkner and Company in 1861. Partners in the firm were Pre-Raphaelite painters Ford Madox Brown, Dante Gabriel Rossetti, Sir Edward Coley Burne-Jones, engineer Peter Paul Marshall, architect Philip Webb, and bookkeeper Charles Faulkner. The diverse group of artists represented in this company produced furniture, stained glass, mural painting, painted tiles, embroidery, metalwork, chintzes, wallpapers, tapestries, and carpets in a variety of styles ranging from Gothic to vernacular (see cat. nos. 1, 120). Due to irreconcilable personal and artistic differences, however, the firm was reorganized in 1875 as Morris and Company, with Morris as the sole proprietor.

A wealthy man through inheritance, Morris had the time and money to devote to this venture. Intrigued by every detail of the design and production process, he devoted hours to the mastery of dyeing, weaving, and embroidery techniques. Morris's medieval furniture designs required a considerable amount of intricate hand labor, including painting and carving. As a result, the prices of these goods were generally high and mainly affordable only for the upper classes.

Warington Taylor, Morris and Company's business manager, was troubled by the expense and elitism of the firm's Gothic-style furniture. He suggested several vernacular chair designs that were plainer, more lightweight and informal, and less expensive than those currently under production. Although Morris preferred the medieval style and resisted the changes, he eventually approved the new designs, which were first produced in 1865. Copied from an eighteenth-century chair manufactured in a Sussex village, Taylor's rush-seated chair (cat. no. 1) was made cheaply for general sale and became one of the best-selling items in Morris and

Company's history. Variants of vernacular furniture, such as the "Sussex" chair and the adjustable, reclining "Morris" chair—also inspired by examples found in the same workshop of a Sussex carpenter—became an integral part of Arts and Crafts production in England, Europe, and the United States (see cat. no. 7).

In 1890 Morris founded the Kelmscott Press to improve the standards of printing and book design. Morris's printing enterprise lasted only six years, but in that short time, he influenced a number of presses in England and the United States (see page 78).

Throughout his career, Morris struggled to harmonize his artistic ideals with his political convictions. His commitment to creating products of the highest design and technical standards constantly undermined his ability to produce them at costs affordable to mass consumers. Finally convinced that design reform was impossible without social and political changes, he dedicated the last decade of his life to the socialist movement.

A host of younger English architects and designers viewed Morris as a prophet and furthered his mission by founding organizations such as the Century Guild (1882), the Art Workers' Guild (1884), and the Arts and Crafts Exhibition Society (1888). Patterned on medieval guilds, these societies provided an environment in which professional and amateur craftsmen could come together for lectures, workshops, and exhibitions. The most notable of these groups was the Arts and Crafts Exhibition Society, from which the name of the artistic movement was derived.

In the early twentieth century, Morris's handicraft revival took root in the United States thanks to numerous craftsmen; two of the most dedicated were Gustav Stickley and Elbert Hubbard (see pages 21 and 30).

1

"Sussex" Chair, from 1865

Morris and Co.

Ebonized beech wood with rush seat

H: 33 1/2" (851 mm)

W: 19 1/4" (489 mm)

D: 16 1/2 " (419 mm)

The Spencer Museum of Art; gift of
    the Friends of the Art Museum,
    76.27

Literature: Aslin, 1962, pp. 55, 58 • Gloag, 1964, p. 256 • Aslin, 1969, p. 30, illus. no. 20 • Naylor, 1971, no. 23, illus. • Anscombe and Gere, 1978, p. 76, illus. • Adams, 1987, pp. 45–47, illus. (color) • Kaplan, 1987, pp. 80–81 • Kaplan, ed., 1989, pp. 53–54.

THE CRAFTSMAN WORKSHOPS (1901–16)
EASTWOOD, NEW YORK

Gustav Stickley (1857–1942) was one of America's most devoted disciples of William Morris and the Arts and Crafts movement. After a visit to England where he was exposed to the design and reform ideas of Morris and other British craftsmen, Stickley formed his own company in 1899. Located in Eastwood, New York, the company was first called United Crafts but was renamed the Craftsman Workshops in 1901. Attempting to promote the artistic and moralistic principles established by Morris, Stickley produced simple, high-quality furniture, metalwork, lighting, and textiles (see cat. nos. 2–7; 9; 13). Stickley chose "Als ik kan" (roughly translated "as best I can"), the Flemish version of William Morris's motto, as the Craftsman Workshops' trademark. In addition to his duties at the workshop, Stickley edited and published *The Craftsman,* a journal that became the most important factor in popularizing the Arts and Crafts ideal in the United States (see cat. nos. 98–99).

Although Stickley's philosophies were akin to those of Morris, his furniture did not resemble that of his English counterpart. Morris furniture was often made of ebonized or colored wood ornamented with carved and painted designs. Stickley's designs, in contrast, were minimal and severely rectilinear with an absence of applied decoration. More direct influences on Stickley furniture included the angular, natural wood furnishings by English Arts and Crafts designer A. H. Mackmurdo and primitive, austere, seventeenth-century colonial furniture.

The Craftsman Workshops constructed furnishings mainly of quarter-sawn oak—one of the most durable woods—finished with fumed ammonia to preserve and emphasize the graining and tonality inherent in the material. The furniture's tenons were often visible, accentuating the strength of Stickley's joined construction technique. Seats and cushions were of leather, rush, or other natural materials.

The success of Stickley's Craftsman Shops inspired the stylistic term "Craftsman," which was used when referring to Stickley furniture and later to his metalwork and textiles. Another term often applied to Stickley's furniture was

2 ➤

Serving Table, ca. 1910
The Craftsman Workshops
Oak with hammered iron mounts
Marks (on bottom of top right
    drawer): Als/ik/kan/Gustav
    Stickley (red decal)
H: 39" (991 mm) W: 48" (1219 mm)
D: 20" (508 mm)
Collection of William A. Stout

This serving table evinces Stickley's Craftsman style. It is boldly rectilinear, solidly constructed, and completely void of structural detail except for the hand-hammered iron drawer handles.

Literature: Clark, ed., 1972, p. 43, no. 45 • Cathers, 1979, p. 58, no. 818, illus. • Cathers, 1981, p. 196, illus. • Bavaro and Mossman, 1982, p. 52, illus.

3

Folding Screen, ca. 1910
The Craftsman Workshops
See color plate 1, page 49

4

Eight-legged Sideboard, ca. 1910
The Craftsman Workshops
See color plate 2, page 49

5

Dining Chair, ca. 1910
The Craftsman Workshops
See color plate 3, page 50

"Mission." Several differing explanations exist for the origin of this term. A popular theory was that the Mission style grew out of a late nineteenth-century fascination with the architecture of the old Spanish missions in California. The simple, straight lines and lack of ornamentation characteristic of Stickley's designs were thought to replicate those in furniture (pulpits, confessionals, lecterns, chairs, etc.) of the missions. An alternative explanation published in a brief note in *The Craftsman,* was probably more accurate.

> The real origin of "mission" furniture is this: A number of years ago a manufacturer made two very clumsy chairs, the legs of which were merely three-inch posts, the backs straight, and the whole construction crude to a degree. They were shown at a spring exhibition of furniture, where they attracted a good deal of attention as a novelty. It was just at that time that the California Missions were exciting much attention, and a clever Chicago dealer, seeing the advertising value that lay in the idea, bought both pieces and advertised them as having been found in the California Missions.
>
> Another dealer, who possesses a genius for inventing or choosing exactly the right name for a thing, saw these chairs and was inspired with the idea that it would be a good thing to make a small line of this furniture and name it "mission" furniture.
>
> (*The Craftsman,* XVI, May, 1909, p. 225.)

Stickley never accepted the use of the term Mission, preferring his own marketing label, Craftsman.

Other American manufacturers, including Gustav's brothers, capitalized on the sudden popularity of Craftsman designs by producing copies that were often made of poorer materials and with less attention to detail and craftsmanship. In response to this competition, Stickley felt compelled to lower the prices of his goods. Violating the edict of Morris, Stickley employed mechanization in his workshops to reduce costs. He justified this decision by claiming it was a deliverance for craftsmen from monotonous labor, permitting them to concentrate on more important detail work.

6

Dining Room Table and Chairs,
    ca. 1910
The Craftsman Workshops
Oak
Mark (on pedestal leg):
Als/ik/kan/Gustav Stickley (red
    decal)
H: 29" (737 mm)
D: 60" (1524 mm)
Collection of William A. Stout

7

Morris Chair, ca. 1909–1916
Attributed to the Craftsman
    Workshops
See color plate 4, page 50

8

Magazine Stand, ca. 1915
Shop of the Crafters at Cincinnati
See color plate 5, page 51

With the aid of automation, Stickley's company continued to prosper. He moved his editorial and executive operations to New York City, while the workshops remained in Eastwood. As if to compensate for this removal from his roots, Stickley purchased land in New Jersey, where a model farm and small family community—similar to the one developed by Roycroft—were planned and partially realized. Stickley eventually overextended his financial empire and declared bankruptcy in 1915. The Craftsman Workshops were taken over by his brothers' rival firm, L. and J. G. Stickley, of Syracuse.

SHOP OF THE CRAFTERS (1904–20)
CINCINNATI, OHIO

Inspired by the popularity of Gustav Stickley's Craftsman designs and contemporary German and Austro-Hungarian furnishings exhibited at the Louisiana Purchase Exposition in St. Louis in 1904, Oscar Onken (1858–1948) introduced his own line of Arts and Crafts furnishings in Cincinnati in the fall of 1904. In his Cincinnati shop, called Shop of the Crafters, Onken attempted to integrate the European avant-garde with his own brand of American Mission-style furniture by enlisting the services of Paul Horti, noted Hungarian professor of design, and by employing a number of skilled German craftsmen. These foreign craftsmen often incorporated colored inlays of wood and tile and applied carving—decorative details borrowed from Austria and Hungary—to animate the straight, simple lines of Arts and Crafts furniture.

Unlike Stickley, Onken refused any machine assistance in his workshops and made his furniture by hand. As a result, Shop of the Crafters furnishings were consistently more expensive than items produced by Stickley's Craftsman Workshops.

TEXTILES

THE CRAFTSMAN WORKSHOPS (1901–16)
EASTWOOD, NEW YORK

By 1910 Gustav Stickley's Craftsman Workshops expanded from furniture production to include the making of metalwork, lighting, textiles, and embroidery. This decision reflects Stickley's desire to create an integrated Arts and Crafts interior. Stickley marketed a variety of textiles, including window curtains, table scarfs, pillow covers, and draperies that harmonized with the color and character of his natural woodwork furnishings. Perhaps the most commonly used fabric was the "Craftsman Canvas," woven of jute and flax and dyed to create an interesting variation of tone. The needlework designs for these fabrics were bold and simple, often consisting of floral motifs. Because the patterns offered by the Craftsman Workshops featured simple stitches and required minimal skill, Stickley sold material stamped with a design for amateurs to embroider at home. (For more on Stickley's Craftsman Workshops, see page 28.)

9

Table Scarf, ca. 1910
Attributed to the Craftsman
    Workshops
Appliqué on linen
L: 53" (1346 mm)
W: 17 1/2" (445 mm)
Collection of William A. Stout

The fabric and stylized embroidered design of this table scarf suggest an attribution to the Craftsman Workshops.

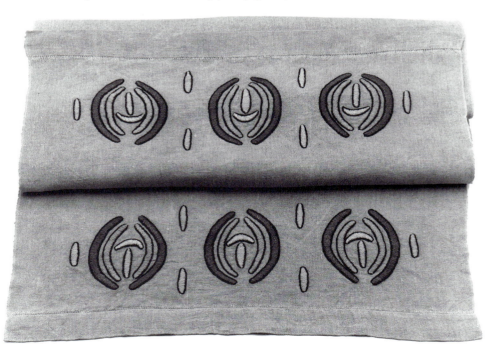

AMERICAN SOUTHWEST—LATE NINETEENTH CENTURY

Native Americans were considered by Stickley and other Arts and Crafts spokesmen to be the original craftsmen of the continent. Indian artifacts and designs were, therefore, sought by Arts and Crafts collectors. Used as rugs in Arts and Crafts interiors, Navajo blankets were admired because they were woven on simple handmade looms. The severe formality of the Indians' geometric patterns and the simplicity of their production influenced the design of Arts and Crafts objects, from Gustav Stickley textiles to Rookwood pottery.

10

Navajo Blanket, after 1860
Red, black, white and gold wool
H: 84" (2134 mm)
W: 56" (1422 mm)
The Spencer Museum of Art; gift of
Stella Aten, 72.85

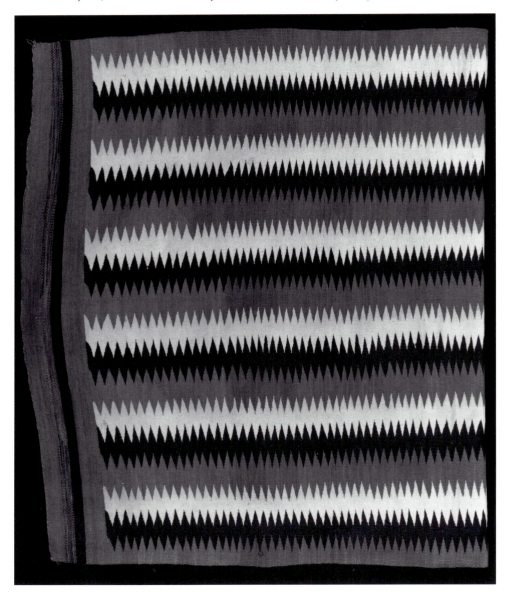

METALWORK

LIBERTY AND CO. (1875–PRESENT)
LONDON, ENGLAND

Founded in 1875 by Arthur Lasenby Liberty (1843–1917) in London, Liberty and Company catered to prominent artists of the day, including James McNeill Whistler, a major figure of the Aesthetic movement; Dante Gabriel Rossetti, a member of the Pre-Raphaelite Brotherhood; and William Morris. The shop offered a unique and fashionable selection of Eastern goods, as well as its own line of silks, embroideries, costumes, carpets, and furniture.

Liberty was sympathetic to the artistic mission of the Arts and Crafts movement, although he rejected Morris's concept of medievalism and idealistic preference for individually crafted objects. In an attempt to reform Victorian decorative tastes, Liberty and Company made beautiful, functional, well-made, and affordable objects with the help of modern manufacturing techniques. Purists of the Arts and Crafts movement eschewed Liberty's commercialism; they thought his designs were being cheaply replicated to meet consumer demand with no regard for pride in craftsmanship.

Although Liberty was severely criticized by some of his peers for relying on machine production, his shop prospered and expanded. He began to stock pieces of English art pottery, including ceramics by Doulton and Company and William Moorcroft (cat. nos. 41–43; 46). This pottery, often designed specifically to coordinate with Liberty and Company furniture, was extremely popular.

Silver and pewter production, which Liberty began in the 1890s, was perhaps the most successful of his ventures. Known as Cymric and Tudric, respectively, the silver and pewter "Celtic Revival" wares were suggested by Welshman John

11

Presentation Cup and Cover, 1901

Liberty and Co.

Designer: Attributed to Archibald Knox (1864–1933)

Silver with enamel decoration

Marks (impressed on base):
Lion Passant (assay mark); upright anchor (Birmingham assay office mark); L and Co.; b; RD.369132

Marks (impressed on lid):
Lion Passant (assay mark); b

H: 10 5/8" (270 mm)

The Nelson-Atkins Museum of Art, Kansas City, Missouri
(F89–31, a-b)
(Aquired through the generosity of Sarah and Charles Koester)

The design of this cup is one of the few that may be firmly attributed to Knox, based on its publication in several contemporary art journals. The cup, decorated with applied cast elements and blue-and-green enamel in a stylized wave pattern, was probably made for Liberty by the firm of W.H. Haseler of Birmingham.

Literature: Victoria and Albert Museum, 1975, p. 56, no. D73 • Tilbrook, 1976, p. 140, fig. 124, illus. • Berman, 1990, p. 188, illus. (color) • Levy, 1986, p. 27, illus. (color)

Llewellyn, Liberty's managing director. Liberty and Company advertised Cymric silver objects as original in form and ornament, adaptable and functional, and individually hand finished. Tudric pieces, made of less costly pewter, were first available in Liberty and Company catalogues in 1902.

Liberty alienated himself further from Morris's commitment to hand production by casting his Tudric pieces in iron molds. This process was followed by a minimal amount of hand finishing. Thus, the hammer-texture surface— usually the telltale sign of human endeavor and craftsmanship—was not actually produced by hand. Ironically, the Tudric line was immensely successful in England and abroad and helped make the style, if not the philosophy, of the Arts and Crafts movement known to an extremely large audience.

A number of artists were involved in the decoration of Liberty metalwork, but Archibald Knox emerged as the company's most valued and prolific designer. Native to the Isle of Man, Knox arrived in London steeped in Celtic tradition and thus was perfectly suited to design Liberty's wares. It is estimated that Knox was responsible for more than four hundred pieces while at Liberty and Company; this figure cannot be verified because the shop neither published the names of its designers nor allowed them to have monograms.

THE CRAFTSMAN WORKSHOPS (1901–16)
EASTWOOD, NEW YORK

Gustav Stickley opened a metal studio at his Craftsman Workshops in May 1902 with the intention of producing hardware for his furniture. As his concern grew for developing a total Arts and Crafts interior environment, Stickley began to make utilitarian objects that would complement his furnishings. Copper, one of the most malleable and inexpensive metals, was the preferred medium. The design of the metalwork, like that of Stickley's furniture, enhanced the natural quality of the material, with the only embellishment being the hammer marks on the surface. (For more on the Craftsman Workshops, see page 50.)

▲
14

Nine-piece Flatware Set with Etruscan Pattern, 1913
Gorham Manufacturing Co.
Sterling silver
Marks (impressed): Pat. 1915; lion; anchor; G; Sterling
H: 9 3/4" (237 mm) [dinner knife]
H: 7 1/2" (191 mm) [dinner fork]
Collection of William A. Stout

....

Created to complement an Arts and Crafts interior and table setting, this flatware exemplifies the simple, geometric patterns often associated with Arts and Crafts design.

....

Literature: Carpenter, 1982, p. 303, illus.

GORHAM MANUFACTURING CO. (1863–PRESENT)
PROVIDENCE, RHODE ISLAND

Founded by Jabez Gorham in 1852, Gorham and Company became known as Gorham Manufacturing Company in 1863. Although it was one of the first silver manufacturers to employ methods of mass production, the firm continued to use handicraft techniques in some of its lines and carried on the tradition of Arts and Crafts design principles.

THE KALO SHOP
CHICAGO, ILLINOIS (1900–70), PARK RIDGE, ILLINOIS (1905–14), AND NEW YORK (1914–18)

Clara Barck founded the Kalo Shop in 1900 after she graduated from the Art Institute of Chicago. Named "Kalo" after the Greek word for "beautiful," the shop specialized in leather goods until 1905 when Barck married George S. Welles, a coal businessman and self-taught amateur metalworker. After her marriage, Clara Barck Welles became interested in jewelry and metalwork, and the couple moved from Chicago to Park Ridge and set up a workshop known as the Kalo Art-Craft Community in their home. The workshop was based on English Arts and Crafts guilds and studio communities. In Park Ridge, Clara Welles and a team of about twenty-five men and women handcrafted a wide range of household metal wares,

◄ 15

Pitcher, 1910–14
The Kalo Shop
Designer: Attributed to Clara Barck Welles (1868–1965)
Silver
Marks (impressed): "Hand beaten at Kalo Shops/ Park Ridge Ills.; Sterling"
H: 8" (203 mm)
Collection of William A. Stout

....

The hammered-texture finish, a salient characteristic derived from English metalwork, and the pronounced simplicity of form and ornamentation—two design concepts underscored in the production at the Kalo Shops—are both evident in this example. The words "Hand beaten" were added to the Kalo Shop's mark in 1910 to emphasize the employment of handicraft techniques.

Seamed construction of this pitcher was likely adopted from the English silverwares produced by C. R. Ashbee's Guild of Handicraft, whose jewelry and silver was exhibited at the Art Institute of Chicago in 1898. The angular design, however, reflects the modernity of Chicago's Prairie School, and the use of a monogram as decoration is a distinctive feature of Chicago art silver—especially of the Kalo Shop. Clara Welles designed the monogram on this pitcher to echo the vessel's contours and its handle.

....

Literature: Darling, 1977, no. 49, illus. (similar example)

▲
16

Compote, ca. 1914

The Kalo Shop

Designer: Attributed to Clara Barck
        Welles (1868–1965)

Silver

Marks (impressed): "Hand Wrought
        at the Kalo Shop; K31OF;
        Sterling"

H: 4" (102 mm) D: 12 1/2" (318 mm)

Collection of William A. Stout

17A, B ➤

Tray, 1925

The Kalo Shop

Silver

Marks (engraved on front—view a):
        Presented to Clara B. Welles /
        The Twenty-fifth Anniversary
        of the Kalo Shop / 1900–1st
        September–1925
        (engraved on back—view b):
        From Kalo Shop Employees /
        Peter L Berg / Arne Myhre /
        Y. Olsson / John S. Cook /
        Wm. Ketter / Robert R. Bower /
        Bjarne O. Axness / Daniel
        Pedersen / Elmer Johansen

L: 19 1/8" (486 mm)

W: 11 3/4" (298 mm)—oval

Anonymous Loan

This unique silver tray was made in
secret and presented to Clara Welles
by her employees on the twenty-
fifth anniversary of the Kalo Shop.
Engraved on the reverse are the
names of silversmiths involved in
making this gift.

Literature: Darling, 1977, pp. 48–49,
129, illus. no. 51

predominantly in silver, for the shop in Chicago. Clara
Welles is credited with the design of most of the wares
produced at the Kalo Shop.

In 1914 Clara Welles left her husband and returned to
Chicago. That year she also established a retail outlet in New
York City, which remained in operation until 1918. Although
she retired in 1940, she gave the Kalo Shop to four employees
and production continued until 1970.

ROYCROFT SHOPS (1894–1938)
EAST AURORA, NEW YORK

Elbert Hubbard (1865–1915) sold his partnership in the
Larkin Soap Company in 1893 and traveled to England in
1894. After visiting William Morris's Kelmscott Press, Hubbard returned to New
York State to establish his own craft community.

Whereas Morris started out crafting home furnishings and later books,
Hubbard began with bookmaking and expanded to produce furniture and
decorative art objects. His printing enterprise, called the Roycroft Press, was
founded in 1895 and published many handcrafted books written by Hubbard and
other well-known authors. Hubbard then established a bindery and a leather shop

to service his press. He proceeded to manufacture furniture, at first to furnish an inn built for visitors to his East Aurora compound. Pleased with his designs, Hubbard began to offer them in Roycroft's 1901 mail-order catalogue. A metal-working shop was subsequently founded to provide furniture hardware and other utilitarian wares. Hubbard's symbol, a double-barred cross enclosing an "R," identified the majority of Roycroft objects.

In 1908 Hubbard hired Karl Kipp, a former banker, to set up an art copper department. Kipp, who conceived most of the designs before turning the prototype over to an assistant, supervised as many as thirty-five men in his workshop.

The Roycroft Shops achieved national fame, and Hubbard's dream of a successful crafts community was realized primarily because of the founder's entrepreneurial talents. Thinking himself a spiritual leader, Hubbard was reborn as "Fra Elbertus" (Brother Elbertus), wearing baggy clothes, shoulder-length hair, and a cowboy hat. Hubbard could only briefly revel in his success; he and his wife drowned when the Lusitania sank in 1915, the same year Gustav Stickley declared bankruptcy. Their son, Elbert II, assumed ownership of the firm but could not sustain it through the depression, and in 1938 the Roycroft Shops were sold.

▲

18

Bookends, ca. 1909–15

Roycroft Shops

Hammered copper

Marks (impressed): Roycroft orb
    (R in circle with cross)

H: 5" (127 mm)

Collection of David L. Stewart,
    Kansas City, Missouri

....

Since bookmaking was the foundation upon which Hubbard built his artistic community, handcrafted bookends were a logical and necessary item to be included in the Roycroft Shops' line of utilitarian copper wares.

◄ **19**

Lamp, n.d.

Roycroft Shops

Copper with Steuben Brown Aurene shade

Marks (impressed): Roycroft orb (R in circle with cross)

H: 15" (380 mm)

Collection of William A. Stout

....

This small copper lamp with a brown glass shade represents a collaboration between Roycroft's Copper Shop and Steuben Glass of Corning, New York (1903–present). The shade is composed of Aurene glass, a form of iridescent art glass developed by one of Steuben's founders, Frederick Carder. (Aurene is derived from the first three letters of *Aurum,* the Latin word for gold, and the last three letters of *schene,* the Middle English form of sheen.) The rich, warm glow of this glass shade was a perfect compliment to the copper base.

....

Literature: Ludwig, 1983, p. 38, no. 82, illus.

TIFFANY STUDIOS (1902–38)
NEW YORK

Although Louis Comfort Tiffany's company came into existence in the late 1860s, its name changed several times and did not officially become Tiffany Studios until 1902 (for more information on Tiffany Studios, see page 37). The company began making metalwork in 1897 when Tiffany organized his own foundry. Featured in its metal showrooms at all times, Tiffany Studios' candlesticks and candelabra were among the most successful products of the firm. Consistent with the principles of Art Nouveau, these objects were often inspired by forms found in nature.

Tiffany's Favrile glass, introduced in 1893, was often combined with metalwork to create decorative household objects such as vases, paperweights, and lamps (see cat. no. 21). This glass, named after the old English word "favrile," meaning "handmade," received a metallic luster from a process involving vapors and gases.

▲
20
Candlesticks, ca. 1902–05
Designer: Louis Comfort Tiffany
    (1848–1933)
Green glass blown into bronze
Marks (impressed on base): Tiffany
    Studios, New York
H: 18" (457 mm)
Collection of William A. Stout

The naturalistic pattern on the base of this pair of candlesticks was known as "Queen Anne's Lace" or "Wild Carrot."

Literature: McKean, 1980, fig. 226, illus.

◄ 21
Bud vase, ca. 1902
Designer: Louis Comfort Tiffany
    (1848–1933)
Bronze with Favrile glass
Marks (impressed on base): Tiffany
    Studios, New York; 711
H: 14" (356 mm)
In memory of Jim Morgan; courtesy
    of the Morgan Gallery

Literature: Koch, 1958, p. 41, pl. 13, illus. • Koch, 1971, p. 114, no. 167, illus. • Duncan, 1981, p. 27, no. 56, illus.

LOUIS SULLIVAN (1856–1924) AND GEORGE G. ELMSLIE (1871–1952)
CHICAGO, ILLINOIS

One of the most progressive centers of the Arts and Crafts movement in the United States was Chicago, home of Louis Sullivan, Frank Lloyd Wright, and George G. Elmslie—architects of the Prairie School. Although Wright is often considered the most prominent of these Chicago architects, Sullivan is the father of the Prairie style. His designs emphasized unity of the exterior with its surroundings and respect for natural materials. Sullivan believed in ornamentation inspired by motifs found in nature, especially plant life.

Sullivan was in charge of the overall design of the Schlesinger and Mayer Company Store (now called the Carson Pirie Scott Store) and is often considered responsible for the baluster panels on the staircase (cat. no. 22). Scholars have convincingly argued, however, that Elmslie, Sullivan's main assistant from 1893 to 1909, designed portions of the building's facade and many of the interior elements. Unfortunately, the documentation of this commission is incomplete and does not provide definitive proof of attribution.

22

Baluster panel, 1899–1901 or 1903–04
Designer: Attributed to George Grant
    Elmslie for Louis H. Sullivan
Copper-plated cast iron
H: 39" (990 mm)
W: 9" (225 mm)
The Spencer Museum of Art; gift of
    the Carson Pirie Scott Store, 80.6

This baluster panel is one of twelve from a staircase once located in the Schlesinger and Mayer Company Store (now the Carson Pirie Scott Store) in Chicago. After a fire in 1967, the panels were removed from the staircase. The Art Institute of Chicago and The David and Alfred Smart Museum of Art (The University of Chicago) own balusters identical to this example.

Literature: Hyland and Stokstad, eds., 1981, p. 136, no. 189. • Mollman, 1989, pp. 173–74, illus.

JEWELRY

▲
23

Necklace, ca. 1910

Designer: John O. Bellis, American,
    d. 1943

Sterling silver

Marks (impressed): Sterling;
    John O. Bellis

L: 10" (254 mm)

In memory of Jim Morgan; courtesy
    of the Morgan Gallery

T HE AIM OF ARTS AND CRAFTS FOLLOWERS to provide beautiful, well-made, everyday objects for the masses led to an alternative fashion in jewelry. Offered at much lower prices than jewelry made from gold and precious stones, Arts and Crafts necklaces, brooches, bracelets, and belt buckles were handmade from sterling silver or brass—the hammer marks are frequently visible—with enamel and semi-precious stone accents. Jewelry designs were often based on natural leaf and floral motifs characteristic of the Arts and Crafts movement. In addition, the style of Arts and Crafts jewelry was influenced by ornaments worn by women in Pre-Raphaelite paintings, which were based on Renaissance prototypes.

Since studios could be set up at home and work was small scale, jewelry making was one handicraft that women artists were able to embrace; they could fabricate as well as design the objects. The Arts and Crafts Exhibition Society, founded in England in 1888, organized special exhibitions for those who worked at home, and many women were able to show their jewelry and receive recognition for their artistic achievements.

Jewelry making was also extremely popular in the United States. Many silver manufacturers, such as Tiffany and Kalo (see cat. no. 28) produced lines of Arts and Crafts jewelry. John O. Bellis was a silversmith trained at Shreve and Company of San Francisco (1852–present) to craft the company's Arts and Crafts wares. In 1906 Bellis decided to open his own workshop in San Francisco where he continued handcrafting silver tablewares and jewelry (see cat. no. 23).

Many surviving pieces of Arts and Crafts jewelry and enamels, however, do not carry any marks or inscriptions that aid in the attribution process. Jewelry made at home was not for commercial purposes and, therefore, did not require or necessitate markings. Likewise, pieces produced by students at art colleges were rarely inscribed with a maker's name.

◄ **24**

Necklace with leaf pattern

American (?), early twentieth
    century

Sterling silver

L: 10 1/4 " (260 mm)

In memory of Jim Morgan; courtesy
    of the Morgan Gallery

▲

25

Bracelet
American, early twentieth century
Sterling silver
Marks (impressed): BH830 S
L: 7 1/4" (184 mm)
In memory of Jim Morgan; courtesy
    of the Morgan Gallery

26 ➤

Belt Buckle
English, late nineteenth–early
    twentieth century
Brass
H: 2 1/2 " (64 mm)
W: 4" (107 mm)
In memory of Jim Morgan; courtesy
    of the Morgan Gallery

27

Brooch
English, late nineteenth–early
    twentieth century
See color plate 7, page 51

THE KALO SHOP
CHICAGO, ILLINOIS (1900–70), PARK RIDGE, ILLINOIS (1905–14), AND NEW YORK (1914–1918)

The Kalo Shop, Chicago's leading producer of handicraft silver table items and jewelry, was founded in 1900 by Clara Barck (Welles). Although the products continued to be sold in Chicago, the workshop, first located in the city, was moved in 1905 to the suburb of Park Ridge. It was organized as a school as well as an Art-Craft community. Many of the silversmiths trained at the Kalo Shop later opened their own studios. (For more information on the Kalo Shop, see page 29.)

◄ 28

Ring
The Kalo Shop
Gold and opal
Marks (impressed): KALO; 24K
H: 1" (25.4 mm)
Anonymous Loan

This elegant gold and opal ring
belonged to Clara Welles, who
probably designed and made it.

Literature: Darling, 1977, p. 129.

STAINED GLASS LAMPS

TIFFANY STUDIOS (1902–38)
NEW YORK

Louis Comfort Tiffany (1848–1933) was an artist of amazing versatility. Recognized primarily for his leaded-glass lamps and windows, he was also involved with the production of paintings, bronzes (see cat. nos. 20–21), enamels, ceramics (see cat. no. 80), and jewelry. Ironically, Tiffany's extremely popular lamps were made from scrap glass fragments that had accumulated during years of window production. These brilliantly colored, handcrafted lamps offered an alternative to pressed glass, which had dominated the market from 1840 to 1860. Often featured in *The Craftsman* magazine as decorative, high-quality objects designed for the domestic interior, Tiffany's lamps contributed to the success of the Arts and Crafts movement. Tiffany was a consummate craftsman, committed to producing art of the highest artistic and technical standards.

The son of Charles Lewis Tiffany, one of New York's most gifted jewelers and silversmiths, Louis C. Tiffany studied painting in Paris from 1868–69. Upon his return to America, he studied medieval glass-making techniques and built his own glass-manufacturing firm, Louis C. Tiffany and Company. From 1879 to 1883, he worked with Candace Wheeler, Samuel Colman, and Lockwood DeForest decorating home and business interiors in New York. Three years later, Louis C. Tiffany and Company was reorganized as the Tiffany Glass Company and received many distinguished commissions, including the public rooms of the White House in 1883. In 1902, the Tiffany Glass Company became Tiffany Studios and produced metalware, pottery, and enamelware as well as leaded-glass lamp shades.

29

Greek Key Table Lamp, 1902–19
Tiffany Studios
Green mottled glass with green and
 yellow leaded glass
Marks (impressed on lower inside
 edge of shade): Tiffany Studios,
 New York #1907
(impressed on bottom of base):
 Tiffany Studios, New York
 #29732
D (shade): 22" (559 mm)
H: 28" (711 mm)—extendable to 35"
Courtesy of Belger Cartage Service,
 Inc., Kansas City, Missouri

While the earliest lamps were made of blown glass, the most popular ones had leaded-glass shades set on bronze bases. These bases were originally designed to contain kerosene, but the advent of electricity allowed a number of new shapes to develop. The shades were made in hundreds of different patterns and colors, many of them with floral designs, and others with geometric shapes. Tiffany continually experimented with glassmaking techniques, striving to produce new textures and colors; he introduced "drapery glass," which consisted of rippled folds, and "Favrile," an iridescent "art glass." He also improved the quality and strength of his leaded glass so that windows and lamps could be constructed with a greater freedom of design.

Flooded with thousands of orders each year, Tiffany and his employees could not make each piece from start to finish by hand. Tiffany relied in part on the machine to cut, grind, and polish the glass, but all the lamps were made under his personal supervision and upheld the handicraft tradition. Simple geometric designs and prominence of green leaded glass made many of Tiffany's lamps perfect accessories for Mission interiors.

30 ➤

Vine Leaf Border Table Lamp, 1902–19

Tiffany Studios

Light-green and yellow leaded glass

Marks (impressed on lower inside
   edge of shade): Tiffany Studios,
   New York #1435–122
   (impressed on bottom of base):
   Tiffany Studios, New York #444

D (shade): 16" (406 mm)

H (base): 21" (533 mm)

Courtesy of Belger Cartage Service,
   Inc., Kansas City, Missouri

Literature: Duncan, 1981, p. 62, no.
170, illus. • Hirschl and Adler, 1989,
p. 59, no. 30, illus.

31

*Geometric Table Lamp on a "Crab"
   Base,* 1902–19

Tiffany Studios

See color plate 8, page 52

32

Daffodil Table Lamp, 1902–19
Tiffany Studios
Yellow and green leaded glass
Marks (impressed on lower inside
    edge of shade): Tiffany Studios,
    New York #1497
(impressed on bottom of base):
    Tiffany Studios, New York #532
D (shade): 20" (508 mm)
H (base): 26" (660 mm)
Courtesy of Belger Cartage Service,
    Inc., Kansas City, Missouri

Literature: Metropolitan Museum of
Art, 1970, no. 272, illus. • Tiffany,
1979, no. 39 (variation of base), illus.
(color) • Duncan, 1981, p. 60
(shade), no. 165, illus. (color); p. 106
(shade), no. 288, illus.; p. 125
(shade), no. 335, illus.

33

Zodiac Table Lamp, 1902–19
Tiffany Studios
Green mottled glass with green
    turtleback tiles and metal filigree
    Marks (impressed on lower in-
    side edge of shade): Tiffany
    Studios, New York #1903
(impressed on bottom of base):
    Tiffany Studios, New York #649
D (shade): 22" (559 mm)
H (base): 15" (381 mm) (extends to
    27 1/2")
Collection of John Belger II,
    Kansas City, Missouri

The shade of this Tiffany lamp comprises six geometrically designed panels. Each panel has a round green
turtleback tile and four horizontal
rows of circular designs made of
metal filigree; the first and third rows
make up the twelve signs of the zodiac.

34

Peacock Table Lamp, 1902–19
Tiffany Studios
See color plate 9, page 52

▲

35

Lotus Leaf Table Lamp, 1902–19
Tiffany Studios
Green and opal-white leaded glass
Marks (impressed on lower inside
    edge of shade): Tiffany Studios,
    New York
(impressed on bottom of base):
    Tiffany Studios, New York
    #28622
D (shade): 25" (635 mm)
H (base): 26" (660 mm)
Collection of Dick Belger, Kansas
    City, Missouri

In a shallow conical shade with an
undulated rim, the delicate lotus leaf
design of this lamp was created with
1,488 pieces of stained glass. The
fluted base has a green doral finish
and is topped with a special finial
design of twenty-four radial ribs
merging into a delicate stem.

Literature: Koch, 1964, p. v, illus. •
Doros, 1978, p. 125, no. 192, illus. •
McKean, 1980, fig. 197, illus. •
Duncan, 1981, p. 67, no. 185, illus. •
McKean, 1982, p. 39, no. 194.

36

Poppy Table Lamp, 1902–19
Tiffany Studios
See color plate 10, page 53

▲

37

Hanging Head Dragonfly Table Lamp,
Tiffany Studios
1902–19
Light-green, green, blue and red
    leaded glass
Marks (impressed on lower inside
    edge of shade): Tiffany Studios,
    New York #1507
(impressed on bottom of base):
    Tiffany Studios, New York #550
D (shade): 22" (559)
H (base): 32" (813 mm)
Collection of Dick Belger, Kansas
    City, Missouri

Literature: Dempsey, 1972, no. 46 •
Toledo Museum of Art, 1978, no. 58
• Johnson, 1979, no. 145, p. 166,
illus. • Duncan, 1981, p. 95 (shade),
no. 259, illus.; p. 278 (shade), no.
278, illus.; p. 106 (shade), no. 286,
illus.; p. 122 (shade), no. 330, illus. •
McKean, 1982, p. 39, no. 196, illus. •
Duncan, Eidelberg, and Harris, 1989,
p. 114, no. 51, p. 115, illus.

38

Lily Cluster Table Lamp, 1902–19
Tiffany Studios
See color plate 11, page 53

39

Wisteria Table Lamp, 1902–19
Tiffany Studios
See color plate 12, page 54

40

Poinsettia Floor Lamp, 1902–19
Tiffany Studios
See color plate 13, page 54

CERAMICS

ENGLISH ART POTTERY

PRODUCTION OF QUALITY CERAMICS was jeopardized by the progress of industry. The machine displaced the individual potter and rapidly yielded inexpensive, poor-quality ceramics. Frustrated by their diminishing role in ceramics production and encouraged by the success of the handicraft revival associated with the Arts and Crafts movement, many potters and decorators escaped the confines of the factory and formed independent studios. Often patterned after medieval workshops, these studios were responsible for reintroducing decorative wares produced entirely or partially by hand.

London was the center for the production of this new "art pottery," and one of the first studios in London was founded in 1873 by the four talented Martin brothers (see cat. no. 44). Within a short time, art potteries appeared throughout England. The outstanding success of these studios encouraged many factories to reorganize their labor forces. Some of the larger, more established firms, such as Doulton and Company, restructured departments to resemble craftsmen studios (cat. nos. 41–43). Minton opened an art pottery studio, separate from its Staffordshire factory, to meet the demand for handcrafted ceramics (cat. no. 45). Many of the "craftsmen" employed by art pottery studios and factories to decorate ceramics were women, and although many received individual recognition for their contributions, they were paid a lower wage than males for the same work.

English art pottery varies widely in style and technique. These ceramics, however, represent the Arts and Crafts pursuit of beautiful, high-quality, handcrafted objects for the enjoyment and benefit of everyone.

DOULTON AND CO. (1854–1956)
LAMBETH, LONDON

Doulton and Company was formed in 1854 by the merger of three family firms, Doulton and Watts, Henry Doulton and Company, and John Doulton, Jr., and became one of the most renowned pottery manufacturers in England. The firm invested profits from its manufacture of salt-glazed, stoneware water and sewage pipes to establish an art pottery. Doulton and Company's first experimental pieces were unsuccessful in technical terms, but by 1873 art studios were opened at the factory and significantly improved wares were produced. Students from the nearby Lambeth Art School of Art, many of them women, were employed to skillfully decorate the art pottery. An enormous range of Doulton wares were produced with incised, carved, modeled, and painted designs, mostly with flower and animal motifs. Many of these pieces were marketed at Liberty and Company in London.

Doulton and Company had a tremendous impact on the ceramic industry as a whole, encouraging potteries throughout England to start art pottery departments. The company ultimately helped bridge the gap between art and industry.

▲
41

Vase, ca. 1910

Doulton and Co.

Earthenware with dark blue, light
    blue, green, and yellow painted
    decoration of stylized trees and
    landscape

Marks (stamp): cipher of Royal
    Doulton / England

Sticker on base: "Richard Dennis /
    Doulton Pottery Exhibition /
    1975/ Part II / 44 B"

H: 8 1/2" (216 mm)

In memory of Jim Morgan; courtesy
    of the Morgan Gallery

....

This ceramic illustrates Doulton and
Company's "barbotine" technique, a
method by which liquid slip is laid
on the ceramic by trailing. Barbotine
ceramics were produced from about
1890 to 1915 and, on a more limited
scale, between 1920 and 1939. The
designs, often stylized trees and
landscape scenes, were hand painted
with colored slips. The decorators
were allowed considerable freedom
when painting the basic designs of
these wares; many of the barbotine
ceramics, therefore, are considered
unique.

Literature: Eyles, 1980, n.p., illus.
(color section)

◄ **42**

Vase, ca. 1902–22

Doulton and Co.

Earthenware with white, black, and
tan painted decoration of trailing
flowers

Marks (impressed): cipher of Royal
Doulton; England; 7919; r; 1029

(incised): FJ

H: 10 1/2 " (267 mm)

In memory of Jim Morgan; courtesy
of the Morgan Gallery

▲
43

Vases, ca. 1902–22

Doulton and Co.

Earthenware with incised design and
    yellow, black, gray, and brown
    painted decoration of stylized
    fruit tree

Marks (impressed): cipher of Royal
    Doulton; England; 7817; 10292; r

(incised): LB

(painted): LB

H: 11" (279 mm)

Earthenware with brown-and-
    yellow painted decoration of
    stylized leaves and fruit

Marks (impressed): cipher of Royal
    Doulton, 10292; 7917; r

(incised): BN; H

H: 6 1/4" (159 mm)

In memory of Jim Morgan; courtesy
    of the Morgan Gallery

MARTIN BROTHERS (1873–1914)
FULHAM AND SOUTHALL, LONDON

Wallace Martin and his brothers, Walter, Edwin, and Charles, began an art pottery studio in 1873. They produced a successful line of ceramics termed "Martinware," a salt-glazed stoneware of unique and varied character. In the spirit of the Arts and Crafts movement, their studio was a cooperative venture, with each brother contributing equally to the production process.

As testimony to his earlier sculpting career, Wallace produced three-dimensional pieces at Martin Brothers. The most famous belonged to a series of grotesque birds, sometimes called "Wallybirds" after their creator. Walter received training at Doulton Pottery at Lambeth before joining his family's enterprise. At Martin Brothers he was responsible for mixing the clay and throwing and firing the pots. Edwin, who was also trained at Doulton, decorated the vases in various patterns. His most common patterns were sgraffito marine patterns, such as spiny-backed fish swimming among seaweed (see cat. no. 44). Charles assumed the role of manager and administrator and was responsible for their retail shop in London.

MINTON (1793–PRESENT)
STOKE-ON-TRENT, STAFFORDSHIRE

MINTON ART POTTERY STUDIO (1871–75)
KENSINGTON GORE, LONDON

Thomas Minton founded a pottery at Stoke-on-Trent, Staffordshire, in 1796, which is still operated by his successors. Many different types of pottery and glazes have been employed by artists at Minton, including earthenware and tableware, wall tiles, majolica, and bone china. In 1871 Minton's Staffordshire firm provided a separate staff and equipment for an art pottery studio. Minton employed William Stephen Coleman, an established illustrator and watercolor artist, to direct the studio and instruct young artists, particularly women, in the decoration of ceramics. Unfortunately, Minton's Art Pottery Studio burned down in 1875 and was not replaced. Wares with Arts and Crafts and Art Nouveau motifs were produced until about 1914 at the Staffordshire Pottery.

Minton's designers embraced the flowing, sinuous lines of the Art Nouveau style and produced an array of ceramics in sizes and shapes that accentuated their patterns. Molds used to form these pots left raised outlines that served as guides for decorators. Since the only hand labor involved was painting and glazing, these wares were relatively inexpensive. During the summer of 1902, the raised slip wares were marketed in a catalogue under the name "Secessionist Ware." (see cat. no. 45.) The name emphasized the impact of contemporary design trends, such as the Viennese Secession movement.

▲
44
Vase, 1898
Martin Brothers
Decorator: Edwin Bruce Martin
(1860–1915)
Salt-glazed stoneware with incised design and blue-and-brown painted fish
Marks (incised): 3–1898; Martin Brothers; London and Southall
H: 8 1/2" (216 mm)

Collection of David L. Stewart, Kansas City, Missouri

Literature: Coysh, 1976, p. 27, illus. (similar example) • Haslam, 1988, p. 103, illus. (similar example)

45
Vase, ca. 1904
Minton Secessionist Ware
See color plate 14, page 55

46

"Pomegranate" vase, 1921–30
William Moorcroft
See color plate 15, page 55

MOORCROFT (1913–45)
STAFFORDSHIRE, ENGLAND

In 1897 William Moorcroft (1872–1945) became a designer in the newly organized art pottery department at James Macintyre and Company of Burslem in the famous Potteries district of Staffordshire. Within a year, Moorcroft had introduced a successful new range of art pottery called "Florian" ware, characterized by Art Nouveau designs. The popularity of these hand-decorated ceramics caught the attention of Arthur Lasenby Liberty, who decided to market Moorcroft's work in his shop in London. Moorcroft was soon producing special pieces to be displayed with the furniture and fabrics of Liberty and Company

In 1913 Macintyre and Company discontinued art pottery and Moorcroft established his own factory, producing many of the old patterns from Macintyre and Company as well as several new ones to be sold at Liberty and Company. By 1919 Moorcroft had become interested in new glazes, especially flambé glazes, created using a copper-reducing technique first perfected by Chinese ceramicists.

PHOENIX WORKS (1883–1959)
STAFFORDSHIRE, ENGLAND

Previously known as Thomas Forester and Sons, Ltd., Phoenix Works was established in 1883 in Staffordshire. The company employed prominent English designers of the day, including Walter Crane. Phoenix Works craftsmen, using glazes and decorations popularized during the Arts and Crafts period, produced an exquisite line of china and earthenware.

47

Set of vessels, ca. 1890
Phoenix Works
Earthenware with brown, dark-
    green, and gold painted deco-
    ration of a peacock in a tree
Marks (stamp): Phoenix Ware; Made
    in England; T.F. and S. Ltd
    (incised): R
H: 12 3/4" (324 mm)
Earthenware with brown, dark
    green, and gold painted
    decoration of a peacock in a tree
Marks (impressed): Phoenix Ware;
    Made in England; T.F. and S.Ltd.
    (incised): 813
H: 7 3/4" (197 mm)
In memory of Jim Morgan; courtesy
    of the Morgan Gallery

ROYAL LANCASTRIAN (1892–PRESENT)
MANCHESTER, ENGLAND

In 1892 the Pilkington brothers began a pottery called Royal Lancastrian at Clifton Junction, Manchester. In the beginning, the pottery produced decorative tiles. Between 1895 and 1897, the company expanded to include art pottery, and many skilled artists, designers, and craftsmen were recruited. The early pots are characterized by simple, elegant shapes and colorful, smooth glazes.

AMERICAN ART POTTERY

FOLLOWING THE LEAD of England and Europe, the United States entered the arena of art pottery production in the mid-1870s. American art pottery had little artistic or technical merit, however, when displayed alongside the richly colored, well-crafted English and European examples at the 1876 Centennial Exhibition in Philadelphia. Inspired by their contemporaries and spirited by the prevailing handicraft techniques of the Arts and Crafts movement, American potters conducted rigorous experimentation, which led to the production of innovative, high-quality ceramics that soon rivaled their international competitors.

The art pottery movement continued to gain momentum, and at the turn of the century, ceramics were being produced in as many as twenty states. Established commercial potteries willing to diversify and expand as well as small studios and workshops flourished in the United States.

The Midwest boasted the greatest number of art potteries. Rookwood started as a small group of female decorators in Cincinnati, Ohio, and became the country's premier pottery company (see cat. nos. 67–78). Other important Midwest potteries were located in Ohio (Owens, Roseville, and Weller, see cat. nos. 66; 79; 86–90) and Illinois (Gates Potteries, see cat. nos. 53–55). Other areas of the country supported innovative art potteries. In Boston, Grueby Faience Company flourished (see cat. nos. 56–58), as did the pottery at Newcomb College, then the women's college at Tulane University in New Orleans (see cat. nos. 59–65), and Van Briggle Pottery Company in Colorado (see cat. nos. 82–84).

The American art pottery movement is characterized by variety and reveals influences from England, other European countries, and Japan. Certain ceramics were admired for their beautiful painted decoration, while others were collected for their distinctive shapes or glazes. Aesthetic concerns were of equal or greater importance than the functional form of the pottery.

48

Vase, ca.1902–03
Royal Lancastrian
Earthenware with blue matt glaze
Marks: Bottom (inscribed) 2967
    Royal, Castrian, England
H: 13 1/2" (343 mm)
Collection of William A. Stout

This example is decorated with a blue glaze developed in 1902–03 that contains zinc oxide and cobalt oxide. A range of wares on which the glaze was used was marketed under the name "Lancastrian" and exhibited for the first time in 1904.

BILOXI ART POTTERY (CA. 1880–CA. 1909)
BILOXI, MISSISSIPPI

George Ohr (1857–1918) learned the art of pottery in New Orleans from Joseph Fortune Meyer, who later worked as a potter at the Newcomb Pottery (see cat. nos. 59–65). In the 1880s, Ohr settled in Biloxi, Mississippi, to raise a family and organize a pottery studio. His one-man workshop soon became a local landmark, and tourists came in large numbers to see if Ohr lived up to the proclamation posted on his front porch: "Unequaled-Unrivaled-Undisputed-Greatest-Art Potter on Earth."

To attract further attention, Ohr fabricated a "Mad Potter" persona, sporting a thick mustache long enough to wrap behind his ears and a beard of such great length that it had to be tucked into his shirt while he worked. The pottery Ohr created was equally eccentric and unconventional. The shapes were often tortuous and twisted, and the glazes were highly experimental and of unusual color combinations.

Although Ohr presented himself as a sideshow attraction, he was well aware of avant-garde trends in ceramics. Some of his pottery bears a striking resemblance to rustic designs of Martin Brothers and to crinkled, asymmetrical pots produced at the Linthorpe Pottery (Middlesborough, England). Ohr likely saw these at the New Orleans Cotton Centennial Exposition in 1884.

Although most of Ohr's pots were made by hand, he produced a number of ceramics that were formed in part by molds. These pieces were inexpensive to produce and sold well. In an unorthodox fashion, Ohr often cast molds directly from objects.

For unknown reasons, Ohr stopped working and abandoned his workshop in 1909. Convinced that the U.S. government would purchase what remained of his work for the national trust, Ohr refused to sell any more of his work. When no offers were made, he stored 6,000 to 7,000 pots in his son's attic; this collection was not dispersed until the early 1970s.

49

Crab holding a fish

Biloxi Art Pottery

Designer: George E. Ohr (1857–1918)

Earthenware

Marks (inscribed): Biloxi, Miss. Art
  Pottery; Geo. E. Ohr; M.D.

H: 7 1/2" (191 mm)

W: 11 1/2" (292 mm)

Collection of David L. Stewart,
  Kansas City, Missouri

This ceramic piece was probably molded directly from a shell and a crab. Additional sculptural details were added by hand.

FULPER POTTERY CO. (1860–CA. 1935)
FLEMINGTON, NEW JERSEY

Fulper Pottery was well established before its line of artware was introduced. The company was producing utilitarian stoneware and earthenware when William Hill Fulper, the founder's grandson, introduced a new line of decorative ceramics made of natural New Jersey clay in 1909. This line was called "Vasekraft" (1909–1929) and included jardinieres, vases, bowls, candleholders, lamps, and bookends. Even

50 ➤

Vasekraft peacock bookends,
ca. 1912–15
Fulper Pottery Co.
Earthenware with bright blue matt
glaze
Marks (stamp): vertical ink stamp
FULPER in rounded rectangle
H: 6" (152 mm)
In memory of Jim Morgan; courtesy
of the Morgan Gallery

more impressive than the range of shapes is the variety of glazes produced by Fulper, including luster, crystalline, matt, and high-gloss finishes in monochrome and polychrome treatments.

In 1910 Fulper added a series of distinctive lamps to the Vasekraft line of art pottery (see cat. no. 52). These lamps were unique in that both the base and the shade were ceramic. On lamps produced by other American potteries, only the bases were ceramic (i.e. Grueby and Rookwood). Over the years, Fulper's Vasekraft lamps have become rare because of the use of electric bulbs with ceramic shades. Continual exposure to the heat of a bulb causes the clay in the shade to become brittle, weakening the support of the glass pieces.

Fulper produced a beautiful array of flambé glazes based on ancient Chinese prototypes (see cat. no. 51). He felt it only appropriate to apply his flambé glazes to classical vessels influenced by Oriental design. These wares were often the most expensive of Fulper's Vasekraft line, sometimes costing ten times more than a matt glaze vase.

▲
51

Vasekraft vessel, ca. 1909–12
Fulper Pottery Co.
Earthenware with tan and gray
streaked flambé glaze
H: 10 1/2" (267 mm)
Mark (stamp): vertical ink stamp
FULPER in rounded rectangle
Collection of William A. Stout

52

Vasekraft lamp, ca. 1910–12
Fulper Pottery
See color plate 16, page 55

GATES POTTERIES (TECO) (CA. 1885–1941)
Terra Cotta, Illinois

In the early 1880s, William Day Gates, founder of the American Terra Cotta and Ceramic Company, expanded his production of tile, brick, and architectural terra cotta to include a line of art pottery. He formed an offshoot company known as the Gates Potteries, which produced a line called Teco ware. The name was derived from the first syllables of Terra and Cotta. Designed without surface ornamentation, Teco pottery was distinguished by its sculpted form. The hallmark of Teco ware was the sea-green matt glaze developed in 1900 and first offered for sale in 1902. Although Teco's glaze was similar to that perfected earlier by Grueby (see cat. nos. 56–57), it was a softer, more even glaze.

Like Van Briggle's vases (see cat. nos. 82–84), Teco ware was produced with molds, making it affordable for more people. The Gates Potteries studio was not widely criticized for using this mechanized technique. In fact, it won highest honors at the 1904 Louisiana Purchase Exposition in St. Louis.

The Gates Potteries, among the first American art potteries established for industrialized production, was a forerunner in the use of designers and technicians rather than decorators to make its ware. Fritz Albert, a sculptor trained in Berlin, was one of these designers (see cat. no. 53). He went to Chicago to participate in the World's Columbian Exposition in 1893. Gates was impressed with Albert's architectural designs and hired him to work at his newly formed art pottery company. Albert created many distinctive pots, ranging in style from Art Nouveau to architectonic.

A French sculptor, Fernand Moreau, also created some unique designs at Gates Potteries (see cat. no. 55). Moreau, who also came to Chicago for the 1893 Exposition, operated his own sculpture studio and taught evening ceramics classes at the Art Institute of Chicago before joining the staff at Gates Potteries.

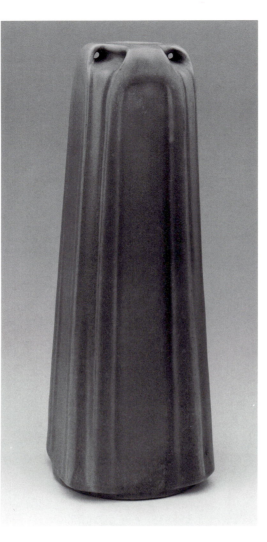

53 ➤

Vase with architectural shape,
    1900–07
Gates Potteries
Designer: Fritz Albert
Earthenware with sea-green matt
    glaze
Marks (impressed): Teco; 184
    (incised): A
H: 14 1/2″ (368 mm)
Collection of William A. Stout

Using a molding technique, the
Gates Potteries produced some of
the most affordable pieces of the art
pottery movement; this vase sold for
seven dollars in 1904.

Literature: Darling, 1989, pp. 122,
142, illus. (color)

54

Squash Blossom vase
Gates Potteries (Teco)
See color plate 17, page 56

55 ➤

Bullet-shaped vase, ca. 1904–20
Gates Potteries
Designer: Fernand Moreau
    (1853–1919)
Earthenware with sea-green matt
    glaze
H: 8 3/4″ (222 mm)
Marks (impressed): Teco, Teco
Anonymous Loan

Although Moreau tended to work in
an Art Nouveau style, this example
illustrates a more linear style.

Literature: Kovel, 1974, p. 264, illus.
• Darling, 1979, p. 62, fig. 69, illus. •
DiNoto, 1985, p. 51, illus. (color) •
American Art Pottery, 1987, p. 93,
no. 51, illus.; p. 89, illus. (color)

COLOR PLATE 1
CATALOG NO. 3
Folding Screen, ca. 1910
Craftsman Workshop
Oak with sheepskin panels
Marks (on base of middle panel):
    Als/ik/kan/Gustav Stickley (red
    decal)
H: 69" (1753 mm)
W (panel): 22 1/4" (565 mm)
Collection of William A. Stout

Literature: Cathers, 1979, p. 79,
no. 91, illus.

COLOR PLATE 2
CATALOG NO. 4
Eight-legged Sideboard, ca. 1910
The Craftsman Workshop
Oak with hammered copper mounts
Marks (on bottom of top second
    drawer): Als/ik/kan/Gustav
    Stickley (red decal)
H: 50 1/4" (1276 mm)
W: 72" (1829 mm)
D: 25" (685 mm)
Collection of William A. Stout

Stickley's eight-legged sideboard
exists in several slightly different
versions. This example does not
have the exposed tenons on the legs
or the square wooden knobs on the
center drawers that were included
on earlier versions. It is not clear
whether Stickley authorized the
alteration in these details or the
designs simply varied over the years
as the cabinetmakers in Stickley's
workshops changed.

Literature: Cathers 1979, p. 53, no.
817, illus. • Cathers, 1981, p. 195 •
Hirschl and Adler, 1989, p. 46, no.
17, illus. (color)

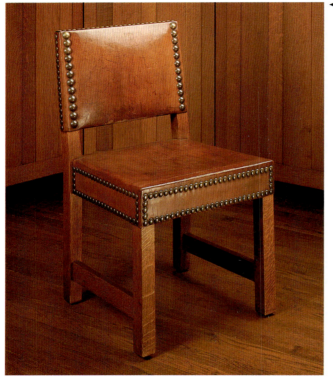

◄ **COLOR PLATE 3**

CATALOG NO. 5

Dining Chair, ca. 1910

The Craftsman Workshops

Oak and leather

Marks (on stretcher):

    Als/ik/kan/Gustav Stickley (red

    decal)

Marks (on bottom of several chairs):

    Craftsman paper label (partial)

H: 33 1/2" (851 mm)

W: 19 1/2" (495 mm)

D: 17 1/2" (445 mm)

Collection of William A. Stout

Literature: Cathers, 1979, p. 60, no.
355, illus. • Gray and Edwards, eds.,
1981, p. 13, illus. • Hirschl and
Adler, 1989, pp. 38–39, no. 10
(chairs), illus. (color)

COLOR PLATE 4 ►

CATALOG NO. 7

Morris Chair, ca. 1909–1916

Attributed to the Craftsman
    Workshops

Oak with fabric cushions

H: 40" (1016 mm)

W: 31 1/4" (794 mm)

D: 36" (915 mm)

Collection of William A. Stout

The Morris chair took its name from
a widely acclaimed reclining chair
introduced by Morris and Company
in 1865–66. In the 1890s it became
one of the most popular American
furnishings for living rooms and
dens in Arts and Crafts bungalows.
Stickley designed seven Morris
chairs, the first patented in October
1901. The design for this example
was printed in *The Craftsman* (XVII,
December, 1909, p. 336) in a section
called "Lessons in Craftsman
Cabinet Work." Stickley often
published his furniture designs so
that amateurs could make the pieces
at home.

Literature: Cathers, 1981, p.130,
illus. • Ludwig, 1983, pp. 60–61,
illus. • Kaplan, 1987, p. 43, illus. p.
383, no. 205; (color)

▲
COLOR PLATE 6
CATALOG NO. 12
Clock, ca. 1915–18
Pewter with mottled blue-and-green
enameled face
Marks (impressed): English Pewter
Made by Liberty and Co.; 01126A

H: 6 3/4" (171 mm)
W: 12 1/2"(318 mm)
D: 3 3/4" (95 mm)
Collection of David L. Stewart,
Kansas City, Missouri

▲
COLOR PLATE 5
CATALOG NO. 8
Magazine Stand, ca. 1915
Shop of the Crafters
Oak, brass, and glass
Marks (original label on back): Shop
of the Crafters at Cincinnati
H: 58" (1473 mm) W: 28" (711 mm)
D: 12" (305 mm)
In memory of Jim Morgan; courtesy
of the Morgan Gallery

This magazine stand was part of a
library set that consisted of a
Viennese clock, a table, and a
Mission desk. According to a 1906

Shop of the Crafters catalogue, all
furnishings in this set were made of
quartered church oak with inlays of
"imported colored Austrian wood." A
choice of wax finishes, such as
weathered, fumed, Flemish,
Austrian, or Early English, was
offered to the customer.

Literature: Gray, ed., 1983, p. 10, no.
336, illus. • Hanks and Peirce, 1983,
p. 94, illus.

▲
COLOR PLATE 7
CATALOG NO. 27
Brooch
English, late nineteenth–early
twentieth century
Silver with turquoise enamel and
beads
H: 3" (76 mm)
In memory of Jim Morgan; courtesy
of the Morgan Gallery

COLOR PLATE 8 ➤
CATALOG NO. 31

Geometric Table Lamp on a "Crab" Base, 1902–19

Tiffany Studios

Green mottled glass with blue and gold Favrile balls and green turtleback tile

Marks (impressed on lower inside edge of shade): Tiffany Studios (impressed on bottom of base): Tiffany Studios, New York #25922; Tiffany monogram

H: 25" (635 mm)

D (shade): 22" (559 mm)

Collection of John Belger II, Kansas City, Missouri

The body of the unusual base on this lamp is made of glass blown through a bronze wire form. The platform consists of three sculptured crabs, one of Tiffany's favorite marine subjects.

Literature: Duncan, 1981, p. 77 (base), no. 207, illus.; p. 96 (base), no. 261, illus. (color)

◄ **COLOR PLATE 9**
CATALOG NO. 34

Peacock Table Lamp, 1902–19

Green, purple, orange, and red leaded glass

Marks (impressed on lower inside edge of shade): Tiffany Studios, New York (impressed on bottom of base): Tiffany Studios, New York #7877

H (base): 26" (660 mm)

D (shade): 18" (457 mm)

Collection of John Belger II, Kansas City, Missouri

The design of this shade includes twenty peacock eyes arranged in two staggered rows surrounded by feathers shifting in color from blue to green. The base echoes the peacock motif; its scalloped platform is decorated with a raised design consisting of six peacock feathers, each with a mosaic eye at its center. A rich patina finish accentuates the design.

Literature: Garner, ed., 1978, p. 17, illus. • Duncan, 1981, p. 76, no. 204, illus. (color)

COLOR PLATE 10 ➤
CATALOG NO. 36
Poppy Table Lamp, 1902–19
Red leaded glass against amber-green
    ripple glass with bronze filigree
Marks (impressed on lower inside
    edge of shade): Tiffany Studios,
    New York #1527
    (impressed on bottom of base):
    Tiffany Glass and Decorating Co.
    monogram
H (base): 22" (559 mm)
D (shade): 20" (508 mm)
Collection of Dick Belger,
    Kansas City, Missouri

Tiffany often based his lamp designs
on floral motifs. The shade on this
lamp is decorated with flowers and
buds of the red poppy against an
unusual background of ripple glass.
Lacelike bronze filigree on the inside
of the leaves produces a realistic
likeness to veins. The base is
stamped with the Tiffany Glass and
Decorating Company's monogram
("TGDCo"), indicating that it was
produced between 1898 and 1902.
The shade was made after 1902.

◄ **COLOR PLATE 11**
CATALOG NO. 38
Lily Cluster Table Lamp, 1902–19
Gold iridescent Favrile glass
Marks (shades): L.C.T. Favrile
    (base): Tiffany Studios,
    New York #333
H: 20 " (508 mm)
Collection of Dick Belger,
    Kansas City, Missouri

An Art Nouveau display, this lamp
comprises eighteen trumpet-form
shades made of iridescent Favrile
glass. The shades rise from a high-
relief bronze base of lily pads, buds,
and blossoms in high relief.

Literature: Doros, 1978, p. 132, no.
190, illus. • Toledo Museum of Art,
1978, no. 59 (floor lamp version),
illus. • D. C. Johnson, 1979, no. 143,
p. 166, illus. • McKean, 1980, fig.
191, illus. (ten-shade version) •
McKean, 1982, p. 39, no. 200, illus.
(ten-shade version)

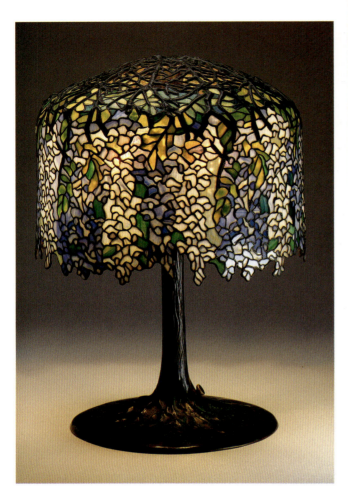

▲

COLOR PLATE 12
CATALOG NO. 39

Wisteria Table Lamp, 1902–19
Tiffany Studios
Blue, light-blue, green and opal-
    white leaded glass
Marks (impressed on lower inside
    edge of shade): Tiffany Studios,
    New York #2267
    (impressed on bottom of base):
    Tiffany Studios #2267
H (base): 27" (686 mm)
D (shade): 22" (559 mm)
Collection of John Belger II,
    Kansas City, Missouri

One of Tiffany's most popular
designs, the Wisteria shade resembles

hanging flower clusters supported by
bronze openwork branches. The
shade is complemented by a bronze
tree-trunk base.

Literature: Koch, 1964, p. v, illus. •
Metropolitan Museum of Art, 1970,
no. 264, illus. • Dempsey, 1972, no.
43 • Doros, 1978, p. 127, no. 194,
illus. • Toledo Museum of Art, 1978,
no. 57 • McKean, 1980, fig. 186,
illus. • Duncan, 1981, p. 238, no.
238, illus.

▲

COLOR PLATE 13
CATALOG NO. 40

Poinsettia Floor Lamp, 1902–19
Tiffany Studios
Red, purple, and green leaded glass
Marks (impressed on lower inside
    edge of shade): Tiffany Studios,
    New York #1528
H (base): 65" (1651 mm)
D (shade): 26" (660 mm)

Collection of Dick Belger,
    Kansas City, Missouri

▲

COLOR PLATE NO. 14
CATALOG NO. 45

Vase, ca. 1904

Minton

Earthenware with relief design and
    dark green, green, white, and red
    painted decoration of floral
    motif

Marks (painted): Minton, Ltd.;
    No. 11

H: 11" (280 mm)

Collection of David L. Stewart,
    Kansas City, Missouri

This example was featured in a
Minton Secessionist Ware catalogue
of circa 1904.

Literature: Atterbury and Batkin,
1990, p. 185, fig. 33, illus.

▲

COLOR PLATE 15
CATALOG NO. 46

"Pomegranate" vase, 1921–30

Moorcroft

Designer and decorator:
    William Moorcroft (1872–1945)

Earthenware with pink, tan, purple,
    and deep-blue painted deco-
    ration of pomegranates; flambé
    glaze

H: 14 1/4" (360 mm)

Mark (impressed): "MOORCROFT"
    "MADE IN ENGLAND" "101"
    (painted green in script):
    "WMoorcroft"

Collection of William A. Stout

Introduced in 1910 at Liberty's,
Moorcroft's "Pomegranate" design
sold in large quantities under the
name "Murena." The pomegranate, a
common Arts and Crafts motif, was
also used in several wallpaper
patterns by William Morris.
Moorcroft's interest in flambé glazes
is exemplified in this elegant vase.
Inscriptions on the bottom of the
pot suggest an approximate
production date of 1921–30.

Literature: Morris, 1989, p. 60, illus.
(similar design)

▲

COLOR PLATE NO. 16
CATALOG NO. 52

Vasekraft lamp, ca. 1910–12

Fulper Pottery Co.

Earthenware with gray-blue matt
    glaze and leaded glass

Marks (stamp): vertical ink stamp
    FULPER in rounded rectangle; 300

H: 16" (406 mm)

D: (shade) 9" (229 mm)

Collection of William A. Stout

◄ **COLOR PLATE 17**
CATALOG NO. 54
Squash blossom vase
Gates Potteries
Earthenware with sea-green matt
    glaze
H: 10" (254 mm)
Marks (impressed): Teco; Teco
Anonymous Loan

Literature: Kovel, 1974, p. 267 (illus.)
• Darling, 1989, pp. 123, 143, illus.
(color)

▲
COLOR PLATE 18
CATALOG NO. 60 (LEFT)
Vase, 1903
Newcomb Pottery
Decorator: Marie de Hoa LeBlanc
    (ca. 1877–1954)
Potter: Joseph Fortune Meyer
    (1848–1931)
Earthenware with incised design and
    blue, blue-green, white, and
    yellow painted decoration of
    stylized centaury plant;
    transparent glaze
H: 11" (279 mm)

Marks (impressed): JM; Q
    (impressed and painted in blue):
    N within larger C [Newcomb
    College]
    (incised and painted in blue):
    MHLeB
    (painted in blue): NN 60
Collection of William A. Stout

As seen in this example, Newcomb
decorators incised simple, bold, stylized designs into wet clay. The piece
was then fired, and the incised design
was painted in a combination of blue,
green, yellow, and black to produce
the most consistent results. The
ceramic was then covered with a
transparent glaze, giving it a glossy
surface.

CATALOG NO. 61 (RIGHT)
Vase, 1904
Newcomb Pottery
Decorator: Sabina Elliott Wells
Potter: Joseph Fortune Meyer
    (1848–1931)
Earthenware with incised design and
    blue, blue-green, and white
    painted decoration of stylized
    water lilies; transparent glaze
Marks (impressed): JM; W
    (impressed and painted in blue):
    N within larger C [Newcomb
    College]
    (incised and painted in blue):
    S.E.Wells (painted in blue):
    YY70
H: 5 1/2" (127 mm)
Collection of William A. Stout

▲
COLOR PLATE 19
CATALOG NO. 75
Vase, 1906
Rookwood Pottery
Decorator: Harriet Wilcox (active
    1886–1907)
Earthenware with green-and-pink
    matt-glaze painted decoration of
    Morning Glories
Marks (impressed): RP cipher (with
    14 flames); VI; 951 B
    (painted): H.E.W.
H; 12 1/4" (311 mm)
Collection of William A. Stout

▲
COLOR PLATE 20
CATALOG NO. 76
Vase, 1912
Rookwood Pottery
Decorator: Sara Sax (active
    1896–1931)
Earthenware with pink-and-purple
    painted decoration of stylized
    peacock feather; Vellum glaze
Marks (impressed): RP cipher (with
    14 flames); XII; 1655D
    (incised): V; V.; SX
H: 10 1/4" (260)
Collection of William A. Stout

▲
COLOR PLATE 21
CATALOG NO. 86

"Rabbit" Vase, ca. 1904

Weller Pottery Co.

Designer: Attributed to Frederick H.
    Rhead (b. England 1880–1942)

Earthenware with incised design and
    green, blue, white, and red
    painted decoration of rabbits in
    a stylized landscape

H: 16" (406 mm)

Mark (incised): "Weller Faience";
    "B463 1/2"

Collection of William A. Stout

Literature: Dale, 1986, p. 38; illus.
(b/w) fig. 42, p. 39; illus. (color)
plate III, p. 70. • Bumpus, 1990, p. 9

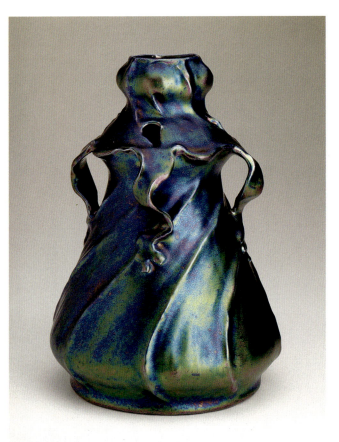

▲
COLOR PLATE 22
CATALOG NO. 89

Sicardo ware vase

Weller Pottery Co.

Decorator: Attributed to Jacques
    Sicard (1865–1923)

Earthenware with blue, purple, green,
    and yellow iridescent glaze

Marks (incised): 11

H: 9 3/4" (248 mm)

In memory of Jim Morgan; courtesy
    of the Morgan Gallery

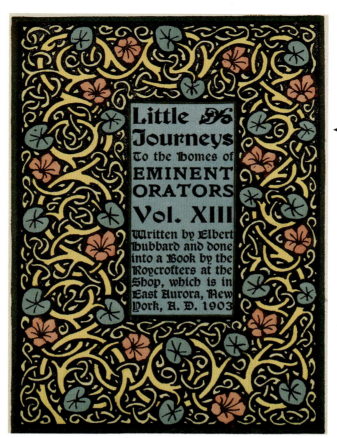

◄ **COLOR PLATE 23**
CATALOG NO. 97

1903 design for *Little Journeys to the Homes of Eminent Orators* (Book II) by Elbert Hubbard

Printed by: The Roycrofters, East Aurora, New York

H: 7 5/8" (195mm)

W: 5 33/4" (146 mm)

Lent by Cynthia and Joe Rogers

Literature: McKenna, 1986, no. 92, p. 113

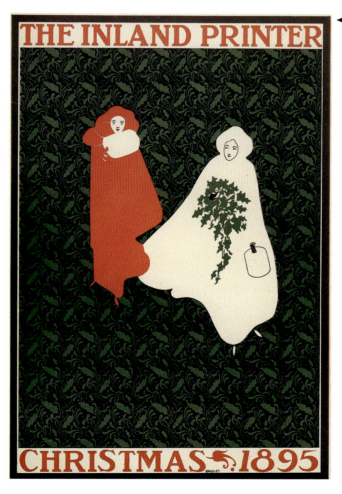

◄ **COLOR PLATE 24**
CATALOG NO. 113

Christmas Poster for *The Inland Printer,* 1895

Designer: Will H. Bradley

American, 1868–1962

Color lithograph

H: 15 1/4" (387 mm)

W: 11" (279 mm)

The Spencer Museum of Art; museum purchase, 70.23

The Christmas issue's unusual design resembles cut-out figures on Victorian wallpaper.

Literature: H. and B. Cirker, eds., 1971, p. 15, illus. (color) • Hornung, ed., 1974, p. vi; no. III, illus. (color)

COLOR PLATE 25
CATALOG NO. 119
Bert's Iris, ca. 1920
Designer: William Rice, American
    (1873–1963)
Color woodcut
H: 12" (304 mm) W: 9" (230 mm)
The Spencer Museum of Art:
    the Letha Churchill Walker Fund,
    90.4

Bert's Iris depicts a bouquet of
irises—a motif repeated in Arts and
Crafts decoration—in a colorful Arts
and Crafts earthenware bowl.
Produced by hand, this woodcut
print embodies the movement's
philosophy, stressing honesty of
materials and emphasizing
craftsmanship.

GRUEBY FAIENCE CO. (1894–1909), GRUEBY POTTERY CO. (1907–13), OR GRUEBY FAIENCE AND TILE CO. (1909–20)
BOSTON, MASSACHUSETTS

William H. Grueby (1867–1925) is credited with the introduction of an innovative matt green glaze in 1897, one of the most significant achievements of the American art pottery movement. Described by a contemporary as having the color and texture of a "fresh watermelon peel," this glaze provided the perfect accent for the oak furnishings of Arts and Crafts interiors. In fact, Grueby pottery was often exhibited with Gustav Stickley's furniture in promotional displays and exhibitions.

The appeal of Grueby's matt glaze lay not only in its color but in its rich, monotone, glossless surface—qualities considered unique to American art pottery. Until that time, dull finishes were achieved either by sandblasting or immersion in an acid bath.

Proudly upholding the Arts and Crafts dedication to handicraft, Grueby's company produced handmade pottery. Each piece was shaped on the potter's wheel and decorated in relief with small ropes of clay. The decoration was done primarily by young women who studied at Boston's School of the Museum of Fine Arts. Grueby's designs were based on leaf and flower motifs, which were well suited for the green matt glaze.

Grueby's matt glaze was admired and widely imitated by proponents of the Arts and Crafts movement, which caused financial problems for the Grueby Faience Company. Grueby attempted to revitalize his business by founding the Grueby Pottery Company in 1907 to produce only art wares. In 1909 the Grueby Faience Company declared bankruptcy. The Grueby Faience and Tile Company was a restructuring of the original company and produced mainly art tiles.

56

Medium vase, ca. 1907
Grueby Pottery Co.
Decorator: Wilhelmina Post
Earthenware with relief design and
  green matt glaze
Marks (impressed): Grueby Pottery /
  Boston U.S.A.; 6/26/7
  (incised): WP
H: 4 1/2 " (114 mm)
In memory of Jim Morgan; courtesy
  of the Morgan Gallery

▲
57

Vase with five handles, 1905–10
Grueby Pottery Co.
Decorator: Wilhelmina Post
Earthenware with relief design and
    green matt glaze
Marks (impressed): Grueby
    Pottery/Boston U.S.A.
    (incised): WP
    H: 9 1/2" (241 mm)
In memory of Jim Morgan; courtesy
    of the Morgan Gallery

Literature: Metropolitan Museum of
Art, 1970, no.286, illus. • Judson,
ed., 1972, no. 140, no. 191, illus. (a
slightly taller version executed by
Ruth Erickson) • Anscombe and
Gere, 1978, p. 166, no. 224, illus. •
Clark, 1979, p. 32, no. 34, illus. p. 33
• Dietz, 1984, p. 66–67, no. 124,
illus. (color) (piece executed by Ruth
Erickson)

▲
58

Tiles, 1906–20
Grueby Pottery Co.
Designer: Addison B. LeBoutillier
    (1872–1951)
Earthenware painted with green,
    blue, and brown matt glazes
Marks (painted): RD
H: 6" (152 mm) W: 6" (152 mm)
In memory of Jim Morgan; courtesy
    of the Morgan Gallery

When these Grueby tiles were first
advertised in 1906, the design was
attributed to Addison LeBoutillier,
an architect who became chief
designer of pottery for Grueby in
1901. These were probably part of a
fireplace frieze entitled "The Pines"
that originally consisted of eight tiles.
Grueby's tiles embodied the Arts and
Crafts philosophy of uniting the
artistic with the utilitarian and were
ideally suited for Arts and Crafts
interiors. Other uses for ceramic tiles,
besides fireplace deco-ration, were
entry hall pavements, bathroom
tiling, and occasionally insets for
furniture or individual decorative
objects set into frames.

Literature: Judson, ed., 1972, no.
197, p. 142, illus. (slightly different
composition and larger dimensions)
• Eidelberg, 1973, p. 48, illus.
(similar design) • Anscombe and
Gere, 1978, p.167, no. 228, illus. •
Bruhn, 1979, p. 26, nos. 58–59, illus.
• American Art Pottery , 1987, p. 81,
no. 42, illus. • Kaplan, ed., 1987,
p. 259, no. 119, illus. (color—similar
example) • Hirschl and Adler, 1989,
p. 62, no. 33, illus. (color)

NEWCOMB POTTERY (1895–1940)
New Orleans, Louisiana

In 1895 Ellsworth Woodward began the pottery program at the H. Sophie Newcomb Memorial College, the women's college of Tulane University. Talented graduates of the art program were allowed to continue to work at the pottery and sell their wares. The Newcomb Pottery studio was patterned on the well-established Rookwood enterprise (see page 66), but the founders took great pride in their Southern heritage and tradition, stressing the use of native clays and motifs.

Because, according to the division of labor at the college, women were only allowed to design and decorate ceramics, men were brought in to throw the wares and apply the glazes. Virtually all of Newcomb's pottery was thrown by Joseph Fortune Meyer, who joined the College around 1896 and stayed until his retirement in 1927.

During the first years of production, the Newcomb Pottery attempted a slip-painting technique resembling that used for Rookwood's Standard ware. The Louisiana climate, however, made it difficult to paint in slip on unfired clay, and workers had to resort to underglaze painting on bisque-fired bodies.

Although Grueby's innovative matt glaze was introduced in 1897, a semi-transparent matt glaze was not used at the Newcomb Pottery until 1910. This new glaze, developed by Paul Cox, caused a distinct change in the pottery style. A new decorating technique was adopted that involved carving naturalistic landscape designs in low relief on the damp body.

Over the years, Newcomb produced several innovative designers, including Marie de Hoa LeBlanc and Sarah A. E. Irvine. De Hoa LeBlanc was one of Newcomb's most accomplished artists of the early period. She graduated from Newcomb College in 1898 and remained to complete her graduate degree in 1901. From 1901 to 1908, she was employed as a pottery worker, and from 1908 to 1914, she served as an art craftsman. Irvine arrived at Newcomb College for the 1903–04 session. She produced some of the finest pottery in the Newcomb style and originated the pottery's most popular motif, a bayou scene with a moon shining through trees laden with moss (cat. no. 63).

59

Vase, 1902

Newcomb Pottery

Earthenware with blue and light-
blue painted decoration of iris;
transparent glaze

Marks (incised): U; McW.
(impressed and painted in blue):
N within larger C [Newcomb
College]
(painted in blue and green): MC
or CM; N 40

H: 9 1/4" (235 mm)

Collection of William A. Stout

60

Vase, 1903

Newcomb Pottery

See color plate 18 (left), page 56

61

Vase, 1904

Newcomb Pottery

See color plate 18 (right), page 56

◄ **63**

Vase, ca. 1914–15

Newcomb Pottery

Decorator: Sarah Agnes Estelle Irvine
(1887–1970)

Potter: Joseph Fortune Meyer
(1848–1931)

Earthenware with relief design and
blue and green painted decoration of cypress and full moon;
semi-matt glaze

Marks (impressed): N within larger
C [Newcomb College]; 229;
J095; JM
(incised): S

H: 10" (254 mm)

The Spencer Museum of Art;
bequest of Ruth Adair Dyer,
89.62

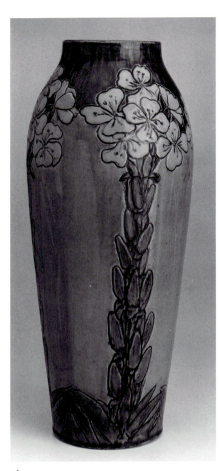

▲
62

Vase, 1904

Newcomb Pottery

Decorator: Hattie Joor

Potter: Joseph Fortune Meyer
(1848–1931)

Earthenware with incised design and
blue, blue-green, and yellow painted
decoration of floral motif;
transparent glaze

Marks (impressed): N within larger
C [Newcomb College]; JM; Q
(incised): HJ
(painted): R 31; HJ

H: 13 1/2" (343 mm)

In memory of Jim Morgan; courtesy
of the Morgan Gallery

64

Vase, ca. 1914–15

Newcomb Pottery

Decorator: Anna Frances Simpson
(active 1908–29)

Potter: Joseph Fortune Meyer
(1848–1931)

Earthenware with relief design and
blue-and-green painted decoration of Louisiana live oak motif;
semi-matt glaze

Marks (impressed): N within larger
C [Newcomb College] : JM;
JL73; 49
(incised): AFS

H: 6 1/2" (165 mm)

The Spencer Museum of Art;
bequest of Ruth Adair Dyer,
89.63

Literature: Ormond and Irvine, 1976,
p. 61 (color-similar example
decorated by Sarah Irvine)

65

Seven-piece tea set
Newcomb Pottery
Earthenware with relief design and
    blue-and-green painted decora-
    tion; semi-matt glaze

Teapot
Decorator: Anna Frances Simpson
    (active 1908–29)
Potter: Joseph Fortune Meyer
    (1848–1931)
Marks (impressed and painted):
    N within larger C [Newcomb
    College]; Q; K; 73
    (incised): JM; AFS
H: 5 1/4" (133 mm)

Creamer and sugar container
Decorator: Anna Frances Simpson
Potter: Joseph Fortune Meyer
Marks (incised and painted):
    N within larger C [Newcomb
    College]; Q; K; 73
    (painted): JM; AFS
H: 4 1/4" (108 mm)

Cups and saucers
Decorator: Anna Frances Simpson
Marks (incised and painted):
    N within larger C [Newcomb
    College]; Q; K; 73
    (painted): AFS
H: 2 3/4" (70 mm)
In memory of Jim Morgan; courtesy
    of the Morgan Gallery

▲
66

Aboriginal form vase, 1907
J.B. Owens Pottery Co.
Bisqued earthenware with painted
    decoration
Marks (impressed): Owens
H: 9" (229 mm)
Collection of David L. Stewart,
    Kansas City, Missouri

J.B. OWENS POTTERY CO. (1885–1907)
ZANESVILLE, OHIO

J.B. Owens Pottery was one of three large potteries based in Zanesville, Ohio. In constant competition with Weller and Roseville, J.B. Owens was responsible for offering a number of original styles of art pottery as well as blatant imitations of lines produced by rival companies. The major line of art pottery at Owens was "Utopian," an imitation of Rookwood's Standard ware.

In 1907 J.B. Owens Art Pottery Company introduced another line in addition to Utopian. Called "Aborigine," this series of wares comprised imitations of Indian pottery in the collection of the Smithsonian (see cat. no. 66). Owens undoubtedly borrowed this concept from Clifton Art Pottery of New Jersey, the first company to produce pottery based on American Indian styles made of unglazed New Jersey red clay.

ROOKWOOD POTTERY (1880–1966)
CINCINNATI, OHIO

With encouragement and financial support from her father, Maria Longworth Nichols founded Rookwood in 1880, naming it after her father's country home. Although Rookwood was created as an outlet for Nichols's creative energies, her first full-time decorator, Albert R. Valentien, and her general manager, William Watts Taylor, soon transformed the small, amateur pottery into a large, professional enterprise.

Early Rookwood production was characterized by a variety of shapes and involved many techniques of decoration that reflected English and French ceramics, especially those popularized by Doulton and Company. Experimentation in the early 1880s led to the development of Rookwood's popular Standard ware, a type of underglaze slip-decorated pottery in which dark brown, red, orange, and yellow colors were covered by a yellow-tinted high-gloss glaze (see cat. no. 69). Rookwood expanded the color selection of its Standard ware in 1884 by introducing the Iris, Sea Green, and Aerial Blue lines, which featured ranges of light blue, green, and gray respectively (see cat. nos. 70–71).

Many unsuccessful and partially successful attempts were made to perfect Rookwood's Tiger Eye glaze. This temperamental glaze was characterized by streaks of golden crystals glowing beneath the surface and was achieved by putting yellow glaze on red clay. Often after a piece was fired, small golden flecks, instead of streaks, appeared beneath the glaze. Rookwood tried to capitalize on this "mistake" and marketed the glaze as Goldstone (cat. no. 67).

As early as 1886, Rookwood artists experimented with matt glazes but did not exhibit the resulting wares until 1901. The company's use of matt glaze was limited compared to other American art potteries (see cat. nos. 72–75). The next innovative glaze by Rookwood was introduced at the Louisiana Purchase Exposition of 1904. Known as vellum because it resembled old parchment, this glaze was neither fully matt nor high gloss. It had a filmy, soft sheen and was used most often with landscape decorations to give an atmospheric effect similar to that of tonal painting (see cat. nos. 76–78). Rookwood continued to produce ceramics until 1966 but discontinued art pottery in the late 1940s.

Without a doubt, Rookwood pottery had the most thorough system of markings of all the art potteries in the United States. Each piece of pottery produced at the studio was marked, numbered, and dated and most were also signed by the artist.

In 1881 Albert R. Valentien (see cat. no. 72) was the first full-time decorator to be hired at Rookwood. He remained in Cincinnati for twenty-four years as one of the company's most talented and skillful decorators. In 1887 Valentien married Anna Marie Bookprinter (see cat. nos. 68; 74), also a decorator at Rookwood. Bookprinter, who studied art in Cincinnati before joining the Rookwood Pottery as a decorator, often accompanied her husband on trips to Europe, where they both came under the influence of Art Nouveau. They eventually began their own art pottery in California (see cat. no. 81).

Nichols eagerly sought to employ Japanese ceramicists, who were admired for their beautifully crafted pieces. Kataro Shirayamadani (see cat. no. 69) arrived in May 1887 and quickly became one of the company's principal decorators as well as a designer of shapes and forms. Shirayamadani remained at Rookwood until his death in 1948.

▲

67

Vase, 1885

Rookwood Pottery

Earthenware with Goldstone glaze

Marks (impressed): ROOKWOOD;
    1885; 242

(Sticker on bottom) Jar from Leeds
    Jar—D. Collomone, Goldstone
    Glaze

H: 6 1/4" (159 mm)

Collection of David L. Stewart,
    Kansas City, Missouri

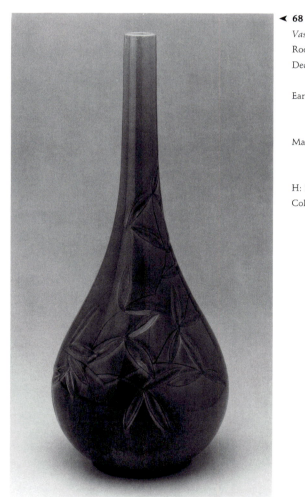

◄ **68**

Vase, 1885

Rookwood Pottery

Decorator: Anna Marie Bookprinter
    (1862–1947)

Earthenware with incised and
    painted decoration and gold
    glaze

Marks (impressed): ROOKWOOD;
    1885; W; 126A
    (incised): AMB

H: 12 1/2" (318 mm)

Collection of William A. Stout

▲
69

Vase, 1890

Rookwood Pottery

Decorator: Kataro Shirayamadani
    (1865–1948)

Earthenware with ochre and brown
    painted decoration of leaves;
    Standard glaze

Marks (impressed): RP cipher (with
    4 flames); 488 F; Y
    (incised): calligraphic mark of
    the artist (Kataro Shirayama-
    dani); 7

H: 11" (279 mm)

Collection of William A. Stout

This baluster-shaped vase by
Shirayamadani is a piece of
Rookwood's Standard ware. The
style was the most popular form of
decoration produced during the
company's early years. Japanese-
influenced ceramics were primarily
decorated with natural motifs, often
of Japanese inspiration. The warm
golden colors and low-relief
decoration of this vase bear a
striking resemblance to Japanese
lacquers.

▲
70

Vase with turkey motif, 1897

Rookwood Pottery

Earthenware with painted
    decoration of turkey; Iris glaze

Marks (impressed): RP (with 11
    flames); 707; A; diamond shape
    (incised): DB (?)

H: 7 1/2" (191 mm)

Collection of William A. Stout

Literature: Cincinnati Historical
Society, p. 123, no. 47.

◄ **71**

Vase, 1908

Rookwood Pottery

Decorator: Charles (Carl) Schmidt
    (1875–1959)

Earthenware with painted deco-
    ration of mushrooms; Iris glaze

Marks (impressed): RP cipher (with
    14 flames); VIII; 905; C; symbol
    for Carl Schmidt
    (incised): W

H: 10" (254 mm)

Collection of William A. Stout·

▲
72

Vase, 1901
Rookwood Pottery
Designer: Albert R. Valentien
    (1862–1925)
Earthenware with purple-and-green
    painted decoration of iris; matt
    glaze
Mark (impressed): RP cipher (with
    14 flames); I; 189 AZ
Mark (painted in black): A.R.
    Valentien
H: 14 1/2" (368 mm)
Collection of William A. Stout

▲
73

Vase, 1901
Rookwood Pottery
Designer: William P. McDonald
    (1865–1931)
Earthenware with incised decoration
    of Indian motif; green matt glaze
Marks (impressed): RP cipher (with
    14 flames); I; 192XZ
    (incised): WMD
H: 17 3/4" (451 mm)
Collection of William A. Stout

Many of Rookwood's early matt
ceramics were decorated with
incised geometric designs resembling

American Indian patterns. The
circular motif of this vase, designed
by William P. McDonald, illustrates
this type of decoration.

Literature: Topeka Public Library,
1880–1980, 1980, no. 76

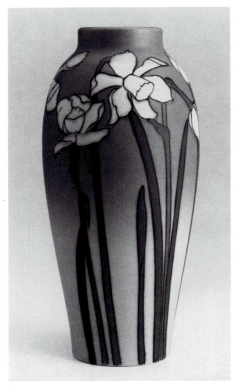

75

Vase, 1906
Rookwood Pottery
See color plate 19, page 57

76

Vase, 1912
Rookwood Pottery
See color plate 20, page 57

◄ **77**

Vase, 1916
Rookwood Pottery
Earthenware with blue-and-gray
painted decoration of landscape;
Vellum glaze
Marks (impressed): RP cipher (with
14 flames); XVI; 2060; V; LMP
H: 7 3/4" (197 mm)
In memory of Jim Morgan; courtesy
of the Morgan Gallery

▲
74

Vase, 1905
Rookwood Pottery
Decorator: Anna Marie Bookprinter
Valentien (1862–1947)
Earthenware with pink-and-white
painted decoration of daffodils;
matt glaze
Marks (impressed): RP cipher (with
14 flames); 901C
(incised): V; AMV
H: 9 1/4" (235 mm)
Collection of William A. Stout

This piece, depicting daffodils with
soft pastel colors in an Art Nouveau
style, was produced in 1905, the year
Bookprinter and her husband, Albert
Valentien, left Rookwood to pursue
their own interests.

◄ **78**

Sunrise, 1916
Rookwood Pottery
Decorator: Edward Diers
(1870–1947)
Earthenware with blue-and-gray
painted decoration of landscape;
Vellum glaze
Marks (recto-painted): ED (verso-
impressed): RP cipher (with 14
flames); XVI; V
H: 8 1/2" (216 mm)
W: 11" (279 mm)
Collection of William A. Stout

As seen in this example, Vellum
ware plaques were often framed for
wall display. The landscape depicted
in this plaque resembles the Ohio
River Valley.

▲
79

Vase, ca. 1925
Roseville Pottery Co.
Earthenware with relief design and
    green, brown, and white painted
    decoration of dogwood flowers;
    matt glaze
Marks (stamp): V within R cipher
H: 6 1/4" (159 mm)
In memory of Jim Morgan; courtesy
    of the Morgan Gallery

Literature: Dietz, 1984, p. 11, no.
230, illus.

ROSEVILLE POTTERY CO. (1892–1954)
ZANESVILLE, OHIO

Along with Weller, Roseville was one of the more successful imitators of
Rookwood. Roseville's early products were similar to Rookwood's Standard wares.
After the turn of the century, however, Roseville began to substitute a relief mold
process for slip-painting on many of its wares. The motifs most commonly used
were floral, and the dogwood pattern was one of the most popular (see cat. no. 79).

TIFFANY STUDIOS (1902–38)
NEW YORK

In 1900 Tiffany expanded his artistic production to include art pottery, but he did
not exhibit examples of these wares until 1904. The application of the Favrile
trademark to Tiffany's pottery implies that it was handmade. Most of the pieces,
however, were cast in molds. In some instances, the molds were made directly
from the copper bodies of his enamels. Despite this mechanical intervention, each
pot was carefully hand finished, and the glazing made each work unique.

Around 1910 Favrile Bronze pottery was added to Tiffany's ceramic
production. This type of ceramic was made by electroplating metal sheathing over
the exterior of the pottery and patinating it. As seen in Tiffany's "Salamander" vase
(cat. no. 80), the surface of Favrile Bronze pottery resembles metalwork more than
traditional pottery. Other versions of this shape exist with a mottled green glaze.

◄ 80

Salamander Vase, ca. 1910
Tiffany Studios
Designer: Louis Comfort Tiffany
    (1848–1933)
Bronze pottery
Marks (incised): L.C.T.; BP 338
    (engraved): L.C. Tiffany Favrile
Bronze Pottery
H: 9 5/8" (245 mm)
W: 6 3/4" (171 mm)
The Spencer Museum of Art;
    anonymous gift in memory of
    Tessie F. and Albert E. Levy,
    89.91

Literature: Loring, 1979, p. 281 •
Volpe and Cathers, 1988, p. 95, no.
60, illus. (version with streaked dark
and pale-green glaze) • Duncan,
Eidelberg, and Harris, 1989, p. 54,
no. 9, illus. (color version with pale
green glaze)

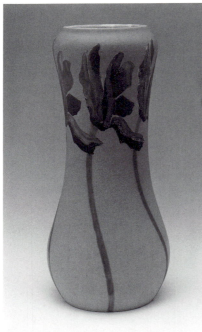

▲
81

Vase, 1911–13
Designer: Albert R. Valentien
    (1862–1925)
Earthenware with green-and-pink
    painted decoration of stylized
    cyclamens; matt glaze
Mark (impressed): VP/Co with
    stylized poppy in vertical
    rounded rectangle; 20'
    (painted): A.R.V.
(Sticker on base): "The Art that is
    Life Exhibition, LA County
    Museum Art 8–13 to 11–7, 1987"
H: 11 3/4" (298 mm)
Collection of William A. Stout

....

Literature: Clark and Hughto, 1979,
p. 74, no. 89, illus.

82 ➤

Vase, 1902
Van Briggle Pottery Co.
Earthenware with green matt glaze
Marks (incised): AA [conjoined in
    rectangle]; Van Briggle; 310;
    1902; III
H: 16 1/2" (419 mm)
Anonymous Loan

....

Van Briggle obtained clays for his
pottery locally, mixing and refining
them to suit the needs of his
company. Early Van Briggle pots

VALENTIEN POTTERY (CA. 1911–13)
SAN DIEGO, CALIFORNIA

Although documentation is scanty, the Valentien Pottery evidently began
operating in about 1911. Albert and Anna Marie Valentien, who met and married
while working at Rookwood, left Cincinnati in 1908 and relocated to San Diego,
California. The move was probably prompted by a commission for Albert to paint
California wild flowers, but once established, the couple also produced pottery.

VAN BRIGGLE POTTERY CO. (1902–PRESENT)
COLORADO SPRINGS, COLORADO

Artus Van Briggle (1869–1904) began working at Rookwood in 1887 and, within
five years, became a senior decorator. In recognition of his achievement,

Rookwood sent Van Briggle to Paris to study painting at the
Académie Julian, an action that underscored Rookwood's
emphasis on painted ceramic decoration. While in Paris, Van
Briggle won a number of awards for his drawings and
paintings, but he remained committed to ceramics. In Paris
he also was exposed to the flat matt glazes of Oriental
ceramics. He returned to Rookwood in 1896 to attempt a
reproduction of this glazing technique. Two years later, Van
Briggle's experiments proved successful. He achieved a matt
glaze effect, much to the satisfaction of his employer.

Van Briggle, however, did not stay long at Rookwood.
Suffering from tuberculosis, which he had contracted as a
youth, Van Briggle was advised to resign from Rockwood and
move to Colorado Springs. In Colorado, he continued to
work with ceramics, trying to perfect a matt glaze for
Colorado clays. Satisfied with the results, he and his wife,
Anne, whom he married in 1902, opened their own pottery.
Their ceramics won national acclaim not only for the matt
glazes but also for the beauty of their shapes. For most of his
ceramics, Van Briggle used a casting method in which a
master mold was created for the original work and casting
molds were made from the master mold.

After the death of her husband in 1904, Anne Van
Briggle ran the company for several years, building a new
pottery in 1908. The company was reorganized in 1910 and
sold in 1912. The current owners kept the Van Briggle name
and continue to produce many of the designs developed
during the early years of operation.

were marked with a Roman numeral
to identify the clay formula. The
incised "III" on the bottom of this
piece denotes a mixture of ground
flint and Sherman clay from the
quarries at Golden, Colorado.

83 ➤

"Lorelei" Vase, ca. 1905–20
Van Briggle Pottery Co.
Designer: Artus Van Briggle
    (1869–1904)
Earthenware with relief design and
    plum-and-blue matt glaze
Marks (incised): AA [conjoined in a
    rectangle]; Van Briggle;
    Colo. Spgs.
H: 10" (254 mm)
In memory of Jim Morgan; courtesy
    of the Morgan Gallery

This piece is among Van Briggle's
most significant works influenced by
French Art Nouveau designs. The
"Lorelei" vase is a sensuous swirl of a
woman's figure flowing into and
emerging from the foundation form.
The original design for this vase was
done in 1898.

Literature: Nelson, 1963, fig. 13 (left)
• Koch, 1964, p. 121, illus. • Clark,
1975, p. 17, no. 13. • Anscombe and
Gere, 1978, p. 158, no. 206, illus.
(color) • Keen, 1978, p. 33, no. 56,
illus. • Johnson, 1979, no. 155, p.
120, illus. • Préaud and Gauthier,
1982, p. 27, no. 40, illus. • Eidelberg,
ed., 1987, p. 48, no. 91, illus. •
Kaplan, ed., 1987, p. 154, illus.
(prototype design of 1898)

◄ 84

Vase, 1910
Van Briggle Pottery Co.
Earthenware with relief design of
    leaves; green-and-blue matt glaze
Marks (incised): AF [conjoined in a
    rectangle]; 1910
H: 4" (102 mm)
In memory of Jim Morgan; courtesy
    of the Morgan Gallery

▲

85

Vase

Wannopee Pottery

Earthenware with dark-green glaze

Marks (impressed): WANNOPEE; 54

H: 12" (305 mm)

Collection of David L. Stewart,
    Kansas City, Missouri

Literature: Trapp, 1990, p. 91, illus.
(similar version)

86

"Rabbit" Vase, ca. 1904

Weller Pottery Co.

See color plate 21, page 58

87 (NOT PICTURED)

Vase with Frog and Snake, ca. 1905

Weller Pottery Co.

Earthenware with green matt glaze

Marks (impressed): Weller

H: 7 1/2" (191 mm)

Collection of William A. Stout

WANNOPEE POTTERY (1892–1903)
NEW MILFORD, CONNECTICUT

Although only in existence for approximately eleven years, the Wannopee Pottery produced some highly innovative ceramics, including "Duchess" ware, characterized by mottled glazes, and "Scarabronze," or lettuce-leaf ware, known for its soft, satiny, metallic glaze suggestive of ancient copper.

WELLER POTTERY CO. (1872–1949)
ZANESVILLE, OHIO

Samuel A. Weller began his ceramics business by making flowerpots and crocks, but he developed an interest in art pottery after visiting the Chicago World's Fair in 1893. An imitation of Rookwood's Standard ware, "Louwelsa" was Weller's most successful line until 1918. Weller followed the Louwelsa line with his own versions of Rookwood's Iris and Sea Green wares.

Perhaps the most interesting ceramics produced at Weller were designed by Frederick H. Rhead (see cat. no. 86), and Jacques Sicard (see cat. no. 89). Rhead, born into a family of distinguished potters, was educated and trained in the finest English art schools and potteries. In 1902 he emigrated to the United States to manage a small pottery in Ohio. In the four prolific decades that followed, Rhead left his mark on the ceramic production of numerous major potteries in the United States, including Weller, Roseville, University City (Missouri), and the Homer Laughlin China Company.

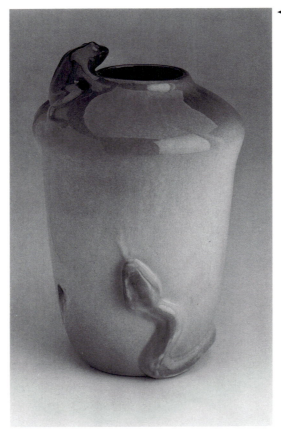

◄ 88

Vase with Frog and Snake, ca. 1905

Weller Pottery Co.

Earthenware with light-green/gray
    gloss glaze

Marks (impressed): Weller
    (incised): Etna

H: 7 1/2" (191 mm)

In memory of Jim Morgan; courtesy
    of the Morgan Gallery

This pot, from Weller's Etna line of pottery, is another version of cat. no. 87 and has been covered with an imitation of Rookwood's Iris glaze.

Literature: Clark, ed., 1972, p. 155, no. 227, illus. • Kovel, 1974, p. 300, illus. • Garner, ed., 1978, p. 192, illus. • Nelson, 1988, p. 23, illus.

89

Sicardo ware vase

Weller Pottery Co.

See color plate 22, page 58

In 1904, Rhead became a designer at the Weller Pottery. The most popular design developed by Rhead while at Weller is known as "Jap-Birdimal" (cat. no. 86). This design is characterized by figures, birds, or animals placed alone or arranged in a simple narrative within a landscape setting. In a display of British wit, this vase depicts a friezelike procession of bespectacled rabbits in jackets hopping in a stylized landscape.

Rhead remained at Weller for only one year, leaving to accept a position as art director at Roseville, also located in Zanesville. Consequently, many of Rhead's Jap-Birdimal designs were produced by others after he left Weller. Although the Rabbit vase does not bear the designer's signature and is not dated, it closely resembles Rhead's style and technique.

Inspired by the popularity of Tiffany's Favrile glass and European iridescent pottery, Weller hired French ceramicist Jacques Sicard in 1901. Working in secrecy to protect his formula, Sicard took two years to develop a successful metallic luster ware named Sicardo (cat. no. 89). The process proved to be intricate and costly, requiring extremely high and dangerous temperatures for firing. Many pieces were destroyed in the kiln. Weller, however, cherished Sicardo ware and continued to offer it for sale even after Sicard returned to France in 1907.

Weller employed a large work force and embraced mechanization. By 1906 his factory ran twenty-five kilns day and night. When Weller died in 1925, the pottery no longer had a sole proprietor, and it became the S.A. Weller Company. Unlike most art potteries, which were forced to close during the Depression, Weller Pottery Company survived and continued production through World War II.

90

Vase

Weller Pottery Co.

Earthenware with incised and light-
blue and purple painted decoration of peacock motif; matt
glaze

Marks (impressed): Weller

H: 13" (330 mm)

In memory of Jim Morgan; courtesy
of the Morgan Gallery

BOOKS

TOWARD THE END of the nineteenth century, technological advances in England and the United States enabled publishers to meet the demands of a burgeoning literate public. While significantly increasing productivity, new power presses, automatic typesetting machines, and photographic reproduction methods severely degraded the quality of printing and dehumanized the roles of printer and designer.

Distressed by mechanical encroachment into bookmaking, William Morris mounted a counterattack against industry to preserve handicraft and elevate the role of printer to fine artist. Although Morris had illuminated manuscripts and designed books earlier in his career, it was not until he heard a lecture on printing at the first Arts and Crafts Exhibition Society in 1888 that he applied his talents to the production of fine books. In 1890 Morris founded the Kelmscott Press, named after his home in Hammersmith, and produced approximately fifty-two books before his death six years later (see cat. no. 91).

Like his early furniture designs (see page 19), Morris's print motifs were inspired by medieval precedents. Illuminated manuscripts and illustrated books, which he termed "pocket cathedrals," served as primary sources of inspiration and were upheld as ultimate examples of the craftsman's genius. In many ways, Morris considered books analogous to architecture—both required a construction process in which separate components or materials had to be integrated into a unified whole.

91

1896 design for *The Works of Geoffrey Chaucer*

Publisher and Printer: The Kelmscott Press (1890–96), Hammersmith

Designer of illustrations: Edward Burne-Jones (1833–98)

Designer of borders and typeface: William Morris (1834–96)

H: 16 1/2" (419 mm)

W: 11" (279 mm)

The Spencer Research Library, The University of Kansas

The Works of Geoffrey Chaucer represents nearly six years of collaborative effort between Morris and Edward Burne-Jones, a lifelong friend and supporter since their days at Oxford. Morris designed the book's elaborate borders, initials, and decorations—all inspired by medieval design—while Burne-Jones drew the eighty-seven illustrations, which were later skillfully trans-ferred to wood blocks. Consistent with his commitment to craftsmanship, Morris arranged for production of handmade paper based on a fifteenth-century Italian prototype.

Literature: Brown Univeristy, 1960, pp. 27–31 • Watkinson, 1967, pp. 57ff • Harvard Univeristy, 1970, p. 12, no. 5 • Banham and Harris, eds., 1984, pp. 209–11 • Kaplan, ed., 1989, pp. 132–33

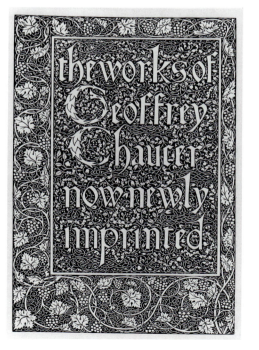

▲
92

1895 design for *Fringilla: Some Tales
in Verse* by Richard Doddridge
Blackmore
Publisher: Elkin Mathews, London
Designer of illustrations: Louis
Fairfax-Muckley, James Linton
H: 8" (203 mm)
W: 6" (152 mm)
The Spencer Research Library,
The University of Kansas

....

Literature: Taylor, 1966, p. 61, illus.
• Harvard University, 1970, p. 35,
no. 36.

The typical Arts and Crafts book produced at the
Kelmscott Press was characterized by crisp, white, handmade
paper; rich, black ink; vellum binding with silk ties or blind-
stamped leather; heavy, often Gothic-inspired typeface; and
woodcut ornaments and illustrations. The title page was
usually a double spread conceived as one unit with decorative
borders and initials. Limited handprinted editions were
produced, often numbered and signed by the artisans
involved.

Morris's press inspired improvements in printing
standards in England and the United States, and bookmaking
achieved a status not known since the Renaissance.
Numerous small presses emerged in the United States
modeled on the Kelmscott, including Elbert Hubbard's
Roycroft Printing Shop in New York State. Hubbard
(1865–1915) visited the Kelmscott Press in 1894. Impressed
with Morris's artistic and philosophical mission, he formed
his own small printing press and craft community in East
Aurora, New York. (For more on Hubbard's Roycroft Shops,
see page 30.) The Roycroft Press, named after a pair of
seventeenth-century English bookbinders, published many
handcrafted books written by Hubbard as well as editions of
works by other authors (see cat. nos. 95–97). In time, Hubbard began to publish
Arts and Crafts periodicals (see page 81).

Hubbard employed many talented designers at his printing shop, but the one
receiving the greatest acclaim was Dard Hunter. After seeing a copy of Hubbard's
magazine *The Philistine* in 1903, Hunter wrote to the Roycroft Printing Shop to ask

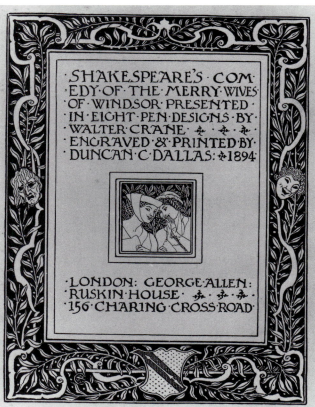

for employment. Although
Hubbard declined, Hunter
persevered, applied for a job
in person, and was hired. He
remained in East Aurora
until 1909, designing books,
metalwork, and glass.
Hunter's most impressive
achievements were his "one-
man books," in which he
provided his own manu-
script, selected the typeface,
designed the layout, and
printed each page on paper
he made by hand.

◄ 93

1894 design for *Merry Wives of
Windsor* by William Shakespeare
Publisher and Printer: Duncan C.
Dallas, London
Designer of illustrations:
Walter Crane (1845–1915)
H: 14 1/2" (368 mm)
W: 10 13/16" (275 mm)
The Spencer Research Library,
The University of Kansas

94 ➤

1900 design for *Pre-Raphaelite Ballads*
    by William Morris
Publisher: A. Wessels, New York
Designer: Helen M. O'Kane
H: 7 7/8" (196 mm)
W: 5 7/8" (144 mm)
The Spencer Research Library, The
    University of Kansas

The influence of William Morris on
this book published by A. Wessels of
New York is two fold—the text is a
reprint of Morris's *Pre-Raphaelite
Ballads*, and the design derives
directly from those printed at the
Kelmscott Press.

Literature: Ludwig, 1983, p. 103, no.
291, illus.

95a

1914 design for *Pig Pen Pete or Some
    Chums of Mine* by Elbert Hubbard
Publisher and printer:
    The Roycrofters, East Aurora,
    New York
Designer of title page, initial letters,
    and decorations: Dard Hunter
H: 7 1/4" (184 mm)
W: 5 1/8" (132 mm)
Private Collection

One of Dard Hunter's best-known
floral designs, this title page was
first used in 1907 for Hubbard's
White Hyacinths.

95b

Leather cover for *Pig Pen Pete or Some
    Chums of Mine*

Literature: Koch, 1967, p. 81, illus. •
McKenna, 1986, p. 140, no. 220

96

1908 design for *Little Journeys to the
    Homes of Great Teachers* (Book I)
    by Elbert Hubbard
Printer: The Roycrofters,
    East Aurora, New York
Designer of title page, initials, and
    tail pieces: Dard Hunter
H: 7 5/8" (195 mm)
W: 5 3/4" (146 mm)
Lent by Cynthia and Joe Rogers

Hunter designed a series published
by Hubbard called "Little Journeys"
(see also cat. no. 97), which was
neither historical nor biographical.
Emphasis was not placed on the text
but on the manner in which the
books were printed. The title-page
border and initials closely follow the
designs seen at the Kelmscott Press.

Literature: McKenna, 1986, no. 163,
p. 129

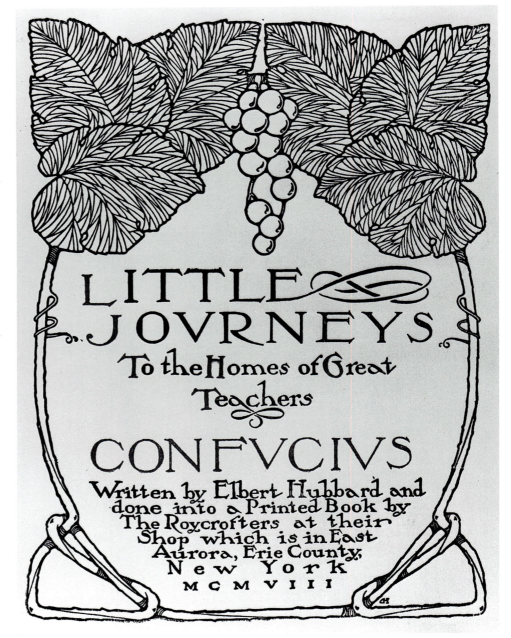

97

1903 design for *Little Journeys to the Homes of Eminent Orators* (Book II) by Elbert Hubbard

The Roycrofters, East Aurora , New York

See color plate 29, page 59

MAGAZINES AND "LITTLE MAGAZINES"

THE POPULARIZATION of the Arts and Crafts movement was largely due to the publication of several magazines. Making their way into many middle-class homes, these affordable periodicals promoted the Arts and Crafts attitude and style with a variety of articles, stories, advertisements, and illustrations.

The major periodical of the American Arts and Crafts movement was *The Craftsman* (see cat. nos. 98–99) established in 1901 by the United Crafts (later to become The Craftsman Workshops) at Eastwood, New York, under the direction of Gustav Stickley. Borrowing its motto from Chaucer, "The lyf so short, the craft so long to lerne," this periodical featured advertisements, technical articles, short stories, and reviews on Arts and Crafts exhibitions. In addition, Stickley published plans for Arts and Crafts furniture and bungalows so that the amateur could become part of the handicraft revival by building his own Arts and Crafts products.

Two other important Arts and Crafts periodicals were published by Elbert Hubbard and the Roycroft Press. From 1894, the year of his company's inception, to 1914, Hubbard produced *The Philistine* (see cat. no. 100), which promoted the Arts and Crafts movement and, more specifically, Hubbard's burgeoning Roycroft Community and Fraternity. The magazine was made of very rough, cheap paper and with little concern for design.

The austere format of *The Philistine* did not attract national advertisers. Hubbard, therefore, began publishing *The Fra* in 1908 (see cat. nos. 101-02). *The Fra*'s format was larger to accommodate advertisers, and it was printed on coated stock to ensure good reproduction of photographs. Designed by Dard Hunter, *The Fra* was more aesthetically successful than *The Philistine*. A membership to the Roycroft Fraternity—available to the public for an annual fee of two dollars—included a subscription to *The Fra* and a book from the Roycroft Press.

Other magazines were dedicated to specific aspects of the Arts and Crafts movement. Beginning as a magazine exclusively for china painters, *Keramic Studio* (see cat. no. 103) became an important periodical for potters involved with the Arts and Crafts movement; it provided technical articles on clays, glazes, firing methods, craftsmen, exhibitions, and awards.

A fad of the magazine publishing industry in the 1890s was the "little magazine." Based on European and English pamphlets, or small books containing tales, short stories, ballads, poems, illustrations, and advertisements that were sold on the streets since the eighteenth century, these magazines were characterized by a small, narrow format. Approximately 225 of these periodicals surfaced and disappeared in the United States during a ten-year period—the 1890s.

One of the first successful little magazines produced in the United States was *The Chap-Book* (see cat. nos. 104-06), begun in 1894 by two Harvard College students, Herbert Stuart Stone and Hannibal Ingalls Kimball, Jr. The magazine was initially intended as a tool to promote their publishing house (Stone and Kimball), but the editors soon broadened its scope to provide a forum for young poets, writers, and artists. *The Chap-Book* appeared twice a month and was a bargain at five cents an issue.

Many prominent designers of the day were commissioned to create illustrations for *The Chap-Book*. Will Bradley (1868-1962) was perhaps the most inventive graphic designer associated for an extended period with Stone and Kimball. Born in Boston, he had rigorous training as a printer before going to Chicago to apprentice as a wood engraver and freelance as an illustrator and designer. Dedicated to the Arts and Crafts ideals of unity of illustrations, graphic design, fine printing, and typography, Bradley published his own little magazine, *Bradley: His Book* (see cat. nos. 107–08), during 1896 and 1897 in Springfield, Massachusetts. Although the magazine was short lived, it was one of the most brilliantly printed of all the little magazines in the United States.

Other artists providing illustrations for *The Chap-Book* included Félix Vallotton, a Swiss artist who contributed several woodcut designs for the early volumes of the magazine, and Frank Hazenplug, an American who designed three posters and a number of Stone and Kimball books as well as numerous illustrations for the magazine.

98

The Craftsman
Vol. XXI, no. 6, March, 1912
Publisher: The Craftsman Publishing
   Co., New York
H: 10 3/4" (275 mm)
W: 8 " (205 mm)
Collection of William A. Stout

The cover of this issue illustrates a typical Arts and Crafts bungalow. In 1904 Stickley introduced the Home-Builders' Club as a service to subscribers. Any member of the club was entitled to receive, free of charge, full working plans and specifications for any of the Craftsman homes illustrated in the magazine.

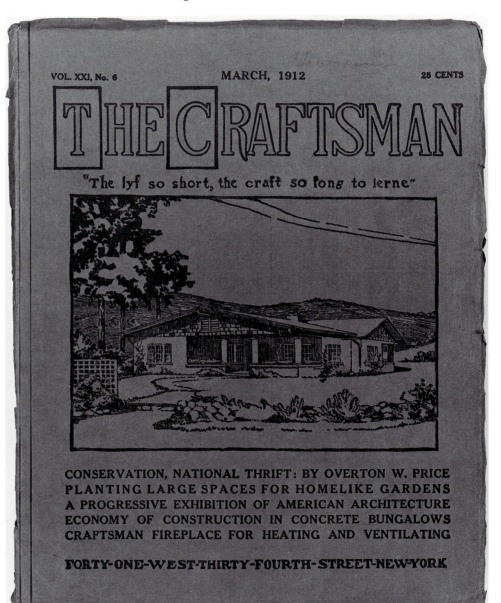

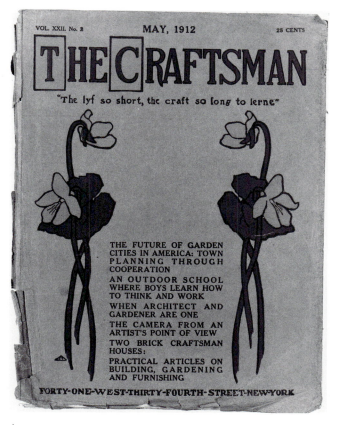

▲
99

The Craftsman

Vol. XXII, no. 2, May, 1912

Publisher: The Craftsman Publishing
    Co., New York

H: 10 3/4" (275 mm)

W: 8" (205 mm)

Collection of William A. Stout

Even though the craze for little magazines lasted only a decade, it reached all regions of the country, including the Midwest. A magazine called *Prairie Dog* was produced in Lawrence, Kansas, and Kansas City was home to *The Lotus* (see cat. no. 109). The debut of *The Lotus* was announced by the Kansas City *Star* on November 15, 1895: "Kansas City now furnishes a recruit to the little army of magazine-lets which has rallied around *The Chap-Book. The Lotus* is its title, and it is a beautifully printed leaflet of which the publishers should be most proud." According to its authors, the magazine was given the name *The Lotus* because that flower was indigenous to the region and was considered by American Indians to be an ancient and sacred flower. Alfred Houghton Clark, professor of drawing and painting at the University of Kansas School of Fine Arts, was one of the artists responsible for illustrations in *The Lotus*.

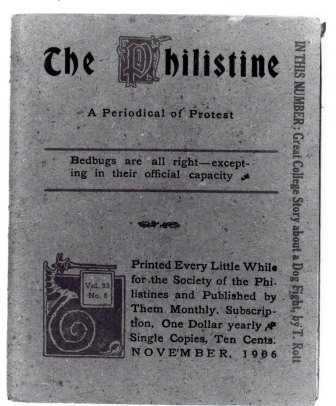

▲
100

The Philistine

Vol. 23, no. 6, November 1906

Publisher and printer:
    The Roycrofters, East Aurora,
    New York

H: 6" (150 mm) W: 4 1/2" (110 mm)

Collection of William A. Stout

Literature: McKenna, 1986, pp.
43–44: 61–65

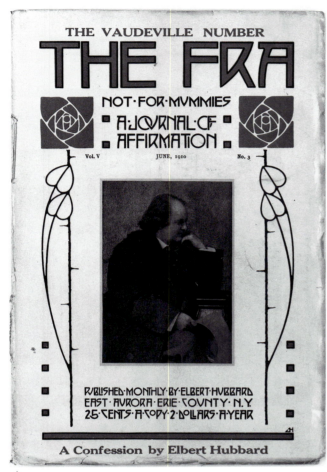

▲
102

The Fra

Vol. I, no. 2, May, 1908

Editor and Publisher: Elbert Hubbard,
　East Aurora, New York

Designer: Dard Hunter

H: 14" (355 mm) W: 9" (230 mm)

Collection of William A. Stout

▲
101

The Fra

Vol. V, no. 3, June, 1910

Editor and Publisher: Elbert Hubbard,
　East Aurora, New York

Designer: Dard Hunter

H: 14" (355 mm)

W: 9" (230 mm)

Collection of William A. Stout

The cover of this issue features a
portrait of Fra Elbertus, otherwise
known as Elbert Hubbard, the
founder and guiding spirit of the
Roycroft Community and the
Roycroft Shops.

◄ 103

Page from *Keramic Studio*

Vol. VI, no. 6, October, 1902

Publisher: Keramic Studio
　Publishing Co., New York

H: 13 5/8" (347 mm)

W: 10 3/4" (273 mm)

Collection of William A. Stout

This page illustrates a design for a
fish plate by Adelaide A. Robineau,
one of the magazine's publishers and
a talented designer of ceramics.

◄ **104**

The Chap-Book
Vol. II, no. 2, December 1, 1894
Publisher: Stone and Kimball,
	Chicago
Designer: Will H. Bradley
	(1868–1962)
H: 7 1/2" (190 mm)
W: 4 1/2" (115 mm)
Private Collection

Literature: Hornung, ed., 1974, no. 5,
illus. (left) • Johnson, 1979, p. 180,
no. 237, illus. • Achilles, 1989, fig.
11, illus.

▲
106

The Chap-Book
Vol. II, no. 3, December 15, 1894
Publisher: Stone and Kimball,
	Chicago
Designer: Félix Vallotton
H: 7 1/2" (190 mm)
W: 4 1/2" (115 mm)
Private Collection

Literature: Achilles, 1989, fig. 1, illus.

▲
105

The Chap-Book
Vol. III, no. 10, October 1, 1895
Publisher: Stone and Kimball,
	Chicago
Designer: Frank Hazenplug
H: 7 1/2" (190 mm)
W: 4 1/2" (115 mm)
Private Collection

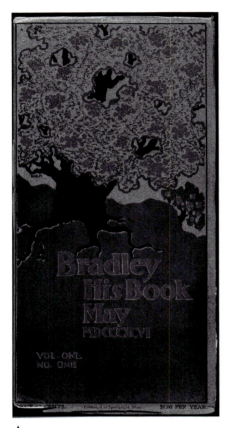

▲
107

Bradley: His Book

Vol. I, no. 1 - May, 1896

Publisher and printer: Wayside Press,
    Springfield, Massachussetts

Designer: Will H. Bradley
    (1868–1962)

H: 9 7/8" (246 mm)

W: 5" (127 mm)

The Nelson-Atkins Museum of Art,
    Kansas City, Missouri (63–35/1)
    (Gift of Mr. and Mrs. George C.
    Dillon)

Literature: Hornung, ed., 1974, no.
31, illus. • Johnson, 1979, no. 262,
p.195

◄ **108**

Bradley: His Book

Vol. I, no. 3 - July, 1896

Publisher and printer: Wayside Press,
    Springfield, Massachusetts

Designer: Will H. Bradley
    (1868–1962)

H: 9 7/8" (246 mm)

W: 5" (127 mm)

The Nelson-Atkins Museum of Art,
    Kansas City, Missouri (63–35/3)
    (Gift of Mr. and Mrs. George C.
    Dillon)

Literature: Hornung, ed., 1974, no.
31, illus. • Thompson, 1977, p. 177,
illus. • Johnson, 1979, p. 196, no.
264 • Kiehl, 1987, p. 110, no. 32, p.
73, illus. (color)

◄ **109**

The Lotus

May 1, 1896

Publisher: Hudson-Kimberly,
    Kansas City, Missouri

Designer: Alfred Houghton Clark

H: 9 1/2" (241 mm)

W: 5 1/4" (133 mm)

The Kansas City Public Library,
    Kansas City, Missouri

Alfred Houghton Clark, a former
professor of drawing and painting at
the University of Kansas, designed
the cover of this issue, which shows
the American Indian with the Lotus
flower.

POSTERS

IN THE 1890s, book and periodical publishers began using posters to advertise new titles or issues. Businesses soon followed suit by commissioning advertisement posters, which were often issued in limited numbered editions like fine prints. A popular item, these posters were the subject of many exhibitions. Journals, such as *Poster Lore* and *The Poster*, contributed to the "poster craze."

The posters of the 1890s represented a tremendous variety of subjects and styles. Some posters depicted characters from a previous time in a striking contrast of black and white reminiscent of the woodcuts and ornamentations of the Kelmscott Press (see cat. no. 110). Others showed figures in contemporary dress in bright color combinations—a style manifested in European posters from the turn of the century (see cat. no. 116). How can these diverse posters be classified together as products of the Arts and Crafts movement? In the same way that William Morris fought for the beautification of everyday objects, poster artists sought to eradicate poorly designed, commercially printed works. Although their styles differed, artists were unified in support of a new fashion of "artistic" poster advertising that called for a higher standard of craftsmanship.

Many artists who were active in other areas of Arts and Crafts graphic design, such as books, magazines, or prints, became involved in making posters. Arthur Wesley Dow, a major printmaker of the Arts and Crafts era, allowed his woodcut design *Sundown, Ipswich River* to be transferred to a lithographic stone to be printed as a poster advertising the first volume of the magazine *Modern Art* (cat. no. 114). This magazine, founded by J.M. Bowles, was important in disseminating the Arts and Crafts ideal. Dow's image represented a simplification of natural forms to emphasize decorative features—a distinctive characteristic of the Arts and Crafts style.

Will Bradley, an innovative book and magazine designer (see page 81), created many posters, including one to advertise Narcoticure, a drug that professed to cure the smoking habit (cat. no. 111), and one to advertise a volume of sentimentalized tales of romance, *When Hearts are Trumps* (cat. no. 112). In 1894 Bradley was commissioned by the editor of *The Inland Printer,* a Chicago-based journal of the printing trade, to design a permanent cover. Bradley's design was so successful that the publisher decided to change the cover each month, a practice that has been followed by magazine publishers ever since. During 1894–96, Bradley created eighteen covers for *The Inland Printer* and various posters to advertise the periodical (see cat. no. 113).

Edward Penfield's posters for *Harper's* (see cat. nos. 115–116), designed during his ten-year tenure as art director, were some of the most popular of the 1890s. Whereas Bradley's style was often similar to that of William Morris, Penfield's art was influenced primarily by French prototypes, including work by Henri Toulouse-Lautrec. The subjects of Penfield's posters, however, were decidedly American. Deeply

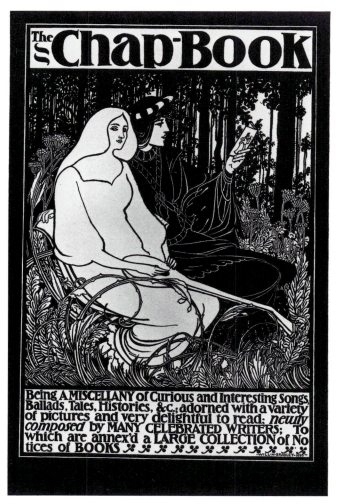

▲

110

The Poet and His Lady, poster for
The Chap-Book, 1895
Publisher: Stone and Kimball,
   Chicago
Designer: Will H. Bradley, American
   (1868-1962)
Lithograph
H: 11 3/4" (298 mm)
W: 7 1/2 " (191 mm)
The Spencer Museum of Art;
   the Letha Churchill Walker Fund,
   70.47

Literature: Johnson, 1971, p. 62–77;
p. 63, illus. • Wong, 1972, cat. no. 5
• Malhotra, Thom, et al., 1973, no.
155, p. 46; p. 57, illus. • Hillier, 1974,
p. 153, illus. • Hornung, ed., 1974, p.
vi; no. 20, illus. • Johnson, 1979, p.
179; p. 181, no. 238, illus. • Kiehl,
1987, p. 105, no. 16, illus. • Hirschl
and Adler, 1989, p. 142, no. 97, illus.
• R. Achilles, 1989, p. 71; fig. 3, p. 69,
illus.

committed to the tenets of the Arts and Crafts movement, Penfield often insisted on supervising the printing of his poster designs to ensure a high standard of quality.

Although her formal artistic training was brief, Ethel Reed became the preeminent female book illustrator and poster artists in the United States (see cat. no. 117). She was renowned for her beauty, and many of the women portrayed in her posters were probably self portraits. Her designs favored female figures surrounded by poppies or lilies in bright color combinations. Reed disappeared in 1898 while vacationing in Ireland and was never seen again.

111

Narcoticure, 1895

Publisher: The Narcoti Chemical Company, Springfield, Massachusetts

Designer: Will H. Bradley, American, (1868–1962)

Color lithograph

H: 19 3/4" (502 mm)

W: 13 9/16" (345 mm)

The Nelson-Atkins Museum of Art, Kansas City, Missouri (F84–78) (Nelson Gallery Foundation Purchase)

Bradley's colorful, well-designed posters revolutionized the advertising of all sorts of products, from magazines to medicines. Narcoticure is based on the medieval theme of Saint George slaying the dragon. In the poster, the dragon is depicted as a prickly-leaved demon in a cloud of smoke. Saint George's impalement of the dragon symbolizes how to "cure the tobacco habit."

Literature: Wong, 1972, cat. no. 25 • Malhotra, Thom, et al., 1973, no. 162, p. 46; p. 47, illus. • Hillier, 1974, p. 170, illus. • Margolin, 1975, p. 44, illus. • Hornung, ed., 1974, no. V, illus. (color) • Kiehl, 1987, p. 105, illus. • Ward, ed., 1987, pp. 244–45, illus.

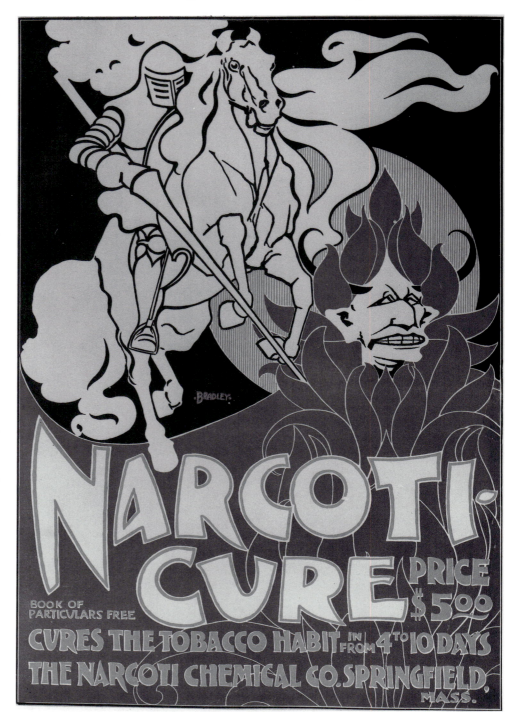

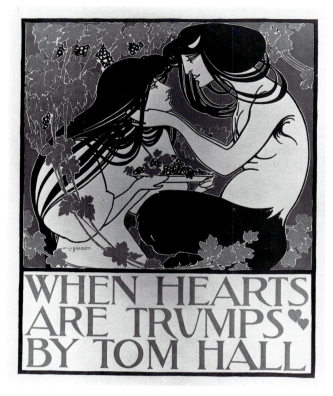

▲
112

Poster for *When Hearts Are Trumps,*
1894
Publisher: Stone and Kimball,
Chicago
Designer: Will H. Bradley, American,
(1868–1962)
Color lithograph
H: 9 7/8" (246 mm)
W: 7 7/8" (196 mm)
The Spencer Museum of Art;
museum purchase, 70.48

One of Bradley's most successful
posters, *When Hearts Are Trumps* was
designed for a volume of sentimentalized tales of romance. Judging
from the compositional and thematic
similarities between this poster and
Edward Burne-Jones's Pre-Raphaelite
painting of *Pan and Psyche* (1878),
the former is probably based on the
latter.

Literature: Koch, 1962, p. 375, fig. 3,
illus. • Johnson, 1971, p. 62, illus. •
Wong, 1972, cat. no. 22 • Malhotra,
Thom, et al., 1973, no. 150, p. 44; p.
50, illus. • Hillier, 1974, p. 148, illus.
• Hornung, ed., 1974, p. xviii; no. II,
illus. (color) • Apostol, 1976, p. 2 •
Hyman, 1978, cat. no. 14, illus. •
Johnson, 1979, p. 165; no. 222, p.
166, illus. • Cirker, 1983, no. 5 and
front cover, illus. (color) • Kiehl,
1987, no. 15, p. 104 • Achilles, 1989,
fig. 9, illus. (color) • Goddu, 1990,
no. 2, p. 67

113

Christmas Poster for *The Inland
Printer,* 1895
Will H. Bradley
See color plate 24, page 59

▲
114

Poster for *Modern Art,* 1895
Printer: Louis Prang and Company
Lithograph
Designer: Arthur Wesley Dow,
American (1857–1922)
H: 19 7/8" (449 mm)
W: 13 5/8" (347 mm)
The Spencer Museum of Art;
the Letha Churchill Walker Fund,
76.40

Literature: Malhotra, Thom, et al.,
1973, no. 217 • Margolin, 1975, p.
103, illus. • Hills, 1977, p. 69, illus. •
Moffatt, 1977, p. 76; fig. 62, p. 79,
illus. • Johnson, 1979, no. 245, p.
183, illus. • Kiehl, 1987, no. 66, p.
119, pl. 4, illus. (color) • Hirschl and
Adler, 1989, p. 143, illus. (color) •
Gengarelly and Derby, 1989, p. 13 •
Goddu, 1990, no. 17, p. 69, illus.
(color frontispiece)

◄ 115

Poster for *Harper's,* March, 1896

Publisher: Harper and Brothers,
    New York

Designer: Edward Penfield,
    American (1866–1925)

H: 18 3/8" (465 mm)

W: 10 13/16" (274 mm)

Lithograph

Collection of Mr. and Mrs.
    W. Bryant UpJohn, Jr.

. . . .

Literature: Malhotra, Thom, et al.,
1973, no. 354, p. 90; p. 91, illus. •
Kiehl, 1987, no. 178, p. 148, illus. •
Goddu, 1990, no. 40, p. 72; Fig. 15, p.
28, illus. (color)

116 ►

Poster for *Harper's,* February, 1898

Publisher: Harper and Brothers,
    New York

Designer: Edward Penfield,
    American (1866–1925)

Lithograph

H: 18 15/16" (486 mm)

W: 13 1/4" (336 mm)

Collection of Mr. and Mrs.
    W. Bryant UpJohn, Jr.

. . . .

Literature: Malhotra, Thom, et al.,
1973, no. 387, p. 100; p. 101, illus. •
Hyman, 1978, cat. no. 12, illus. •
Gibson, 1984, p. 27, illus. • Kiehl,
1987, p. 157, no. 207, illus.

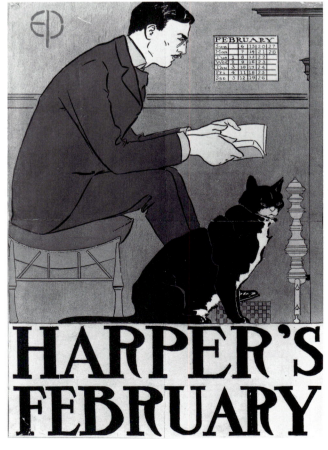

117
Poster for *Folly or Saintliness,* 1895
Publisher: Lamson, Wolffe and Co.,
    Boston
Designer: Ethel Reed, American
    (1876–?)
Lithograph
H: 20 3/16" (513 mm)
W: 14 7/8" (378 mm)
The Nelson-Atkins Museum of Art,
    Kansas City, Missouri (F84–79)
    (Nelson Gallery Foundation
    Purchase)

Literature: Breitenbach, 1962, p. 30,
illus. • Margolin, 1975, p. 169, illus.
• Hills, 1977, p. 63, illus. • Kiehl,
1987, p. 166, no. 239, illus.

PRINTS AND DRAWINGS

EXTENDING TO ALL AREAS of the graphic arts, the Arts and Crafts movement had an impact on prints and drawings of the period. Many printmakers denounced commercial methods, which often involved photomechanical reproduction. The Arts and Crafts movement offered a viable solution to the problems of printmaking. The movement's emphasis on craftsmanship revitalized the use of the woodcut, the simplest and most natural printing technique.

William Morris employed woodcuts extensively for his book illustrations (see cat. no. 118) and decorative wallpapers produced by Morris and Company (see cat. no. 120). In the United States, the interest in woodcuts was partly due to the fascination with Japanese art, specifically woodblock prints. The simplicity and refinement of color and form in Japanese woodcuts was emulated by numerous American printmakers, including William Rice (see cat. no. 119). Rice was born in Pennsylvania and studied at the Pennsylvania Museum of Industrial Art and Drexel Institute before moving to the West Coast. There he continued his printmaking studies at the California College of Arts and Crafts in Oakland. An educator and author of books on woodblock printing, Rice produced a number of woodcuts, ranging from florals to landscapes of the West Coast. He was undoubtedly familiar with articles on Japanese color woodcuts that frequently appeared in *The Craftsman* and other Arts and Crafts publications.

Drawings also reflected the impact of the Arts and Crafts movement on design. Many preparatory drawings or studies for stained glass windows have survived that illustrate the process by which artists developed large, decorative schemes (see cat. nos. 121-22). Windows were inspired by William Morris's medievalism and the rebirth of Gothic architecture.

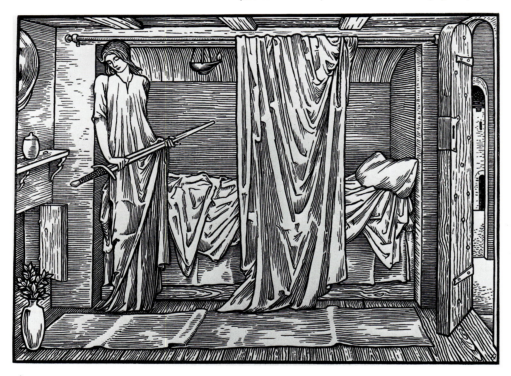

▲

118

Lucretia from the Kelmscott *Chaucer,*
1896

Publisher and printer: The Kelmscott
   Press

Designer: Edward Burne-Jones,
   English (1833–98)

Hammersmith, England

Woodcut

H: 7 1/2" (191 mm)

W: 8 1/4" (210 mm)

The Spencer Museum of Art; the
   Letha Churchill Walker Fund,
   78.108

This woodcut illustration was
designed by Edward Burne-Jones for

the Kelmscott *Chaucer* (see cat. no.
91); the impression was taken before
text and ornamentation were added.

119

Bert's Iris, ca. 1920

William Rice

See color plate 25, page 60

MORRIS AND CO. (1875–1940)
LONDON, ENGLAND

William Morris introduced a line of wallpaper for customers who could not afford to decorate with expensive medieval tapestries and embroideries made by his firm. The line, consisting of more than sixty wallpaper patterns, was one of the most successful of his design ventures.

Initially, Morris supervised production of handprinted wallpapers and fabrics. Producing wallpaper, however, was too arduous and time consuming for his workshop. From 1864 onward, Jeffrey and Company, London, printed all of Morris's wallpaper designs, although the papers were still marked "Morris and Co."

Authentic Morris papers were available in the United States as early as 1873. By the 1880s, Morris and Company wallpaper was common in American homes, and imitations of Morrisean designs were produced in great quantities. Today Morris wallpapers are still handprinted from wooden blocks by the English firm Arthur Sanderson and Sons, Ltd.

120

Double Bough, designed in 1890;
    printed prior to 1905

Morris and Co.

Designer: William Morris, English
    (1834–96)

Block print

Marks: MORRIS and CO.

H: 22 1/4" (564 mm)

W: 41 1/4" (1048 mm)

The Spencer Museum of Art,
    the Letha Churchill Walker Fund,
    89.23

This pastel pattern was printed by hand from approximately ten separate woodblocks. The naturalistic floral design may have been inspired by woodcut illustrations of early printed herbals or flowers in medieval Flemish tapestries.

Literature: Thompson, 1977, p. 108 • Oman and Hamilton, 1982, p. 375, no. 1065, illus. • Nylander, Redmond, and Sander, 1986, p. 240, illus. (color) on back cover

Enthusiasm for medieval models and neo-Gothic architecture, first seen in Ruskin's writings and Morris's designs, led to a national program for the restoration of many original English Gothic churches and construction of many new churches. Several firms, including Heaton, Butler and Bayne (London and New York), specialized in the production of Gothic stained-glass windows for churches. American designers also instigated a rebirth of medieval architecture and design. Production of stained glass for American churches resulted from this medieval revival and embodied the Arts and Crafts ideal. Before work began on a stained glass window, the designer would present a drawing of the design to the patron for approval (see cat. no. 121-22).

John LaFarge was a seminal figure in the development of American stained glass. After beginning his career as a landscape and still-life painter, LaFarge started designing murals and stained-glass windows in 1875. He headed a thriving studio where artists served as apprentices in the Renaissance studio tradition. Besides designing windows, LaFarge helped select glass and hand produce each window. He developed, among other things, a new technique of "plating" whereby glass pieces of contrasting textures were superimposed for special light effects. (For an article titled "John LaFarge, The Craftsman," see *The Craftsman,* XIX, January, 1911, no. 4.)

121

Design for stained glass window:
    The Resurrection, ca. 1890
Designer: Heaton, Butler, and Bayne,
    London and New York
Watercolor and ink on paper
H: 8 9/16" (217 mm)
W: 2 1/8" (57 mm)
The Spencer Museum of Art;
    museum purchase, 70.47

Literature: Wooden, 1983, p. 37,
    fig. 96, illus.

122

Designs for stained glass windows

Designer: John LaFarge, American
(1835–1910)

Watercolors

Left (00.166)—H: 10 1/2" (267 mm)
W: 9 3/4" (248 mm)

Center (00.167)—H: 10 3/4"
(273 mm)
W: 3 3/4" (95 mm)

Right (00.169)—H: 10" (254 mm)
W: 2" (51 mm)

The Spencer Museum of Art;
the William Bridges Thayer
Memorial, 00.166–00.168

These drawings by LaFarge are
separate studies from three different
window commissions. LaFarge's
drawing of a contemplative figure
standing with hands clasped in
prayer (at left) is a color study for
the Frank Semple Memorial Window
in the Presbyterian Church of
Sewickley in Pennsylvania. Situated
in the east wall of the apse, LaFarge's
window bears the date 1908. No
evidence of the windows for which
the other two studies were made has
been found.

123

Qa' Hila-Koprino, 1914

Edward Sheriff Curtis, American

    (1868-1952)

Photogravure

H: 15 1/6" (383 mm)

   W: 11 1/2" (292 mm)

The Spencer Museum of Art;

   museum purchase, 75.39

PHOTOGRAPHS

ALTHOUGH IT SEEMS PARADOXICAL to include photography, a mechanical method of reproducing images, alongside objects made as a reaction against the machine, photographers were equally as concerned about craftsmanship and aesthetics as Arts and Crafts furniture makers and ceramicists. Just as turn-of-the-century designers and craftsmen were striving to have their work accepted as "fine art," photographers were also aiming to be ranked as artists.

Photography was included as a category in general Arts and Crafts exhibitions. Alfred Stieglitz and Gertrude Käsebier, for example, were among photographers whose work appeared in the 1899 Arts and Crafts exhibition at the Society of Arts and Crafts in Boston. The work of these photographers exemplified a fastidious technique and an emphasis on craftmanship. Käsebier, like many photographers, tried to compensate for the photograph's inherent mechanical qualities by opting for rich tonal or pictorial effects (see cat. nos. 127–128). Steiglitz worked to establish photography as a medium of artistic expression and founded a magazine, *Camera Work (*1903–17) to promote his cause. In this journal, Steiglitz published a wide range of contemporary photographs, from those with rich tonal qualities and pictorial effects to nature "snapshots." He helped elevate the status of photography by providing critical analyses and explanations of these images.

The Craftsman magazine also frequently published illustrated articles about pictorial photography, often featuring the work of an individual photographer. Baron Adolph de Meyer's work (see cat. no. 124) was the subject of several articles in the magazine. His still-life photographs were featured in the August 1914 edition (XXVI, no. 5, pp. 517–23). Many of Edward S. Curtis's photographs (see cat. no. 123) were used to illustrate articles on the routines and rituals of various Indian tribes published in *The Craftsman* (for example, see *The Craftsman,* April-September, 1907, pp. 16–33; 269–85).

Alvin L. Coburn was another photographer who firmly believed that photography was a fine art and should take its place in the traditional graphic arts. He thought this could be achieved by maintaining a commitment to craftsmanship. Coburn studied with Frank Brangwyn, an etcher-illustrator who, in his youth, had trained with William Morris. Coburn was extremely dedicated to craftsmanship. For a brief time he manufactured his own gum bichromate paper and, throughout his career, printed his own photogravures. Many of Coburn's photographs were included in Stieglitz's *Camera Work. The Ferry* (cat. no. 126), was featured in the February 1911 edition of *The Craftsman* (XIX, no. 5, p. 467).

124 ➤

Still Life (Water lilies), 1908
Baron Adolph de Meyer, American
   (1886-1946)
Platinum print
H: 6 7/16 (163 mm)
W: 8 3/4" (223 mm)
The Spencer Museum of Art; gift of
   Jack and Connie Glenn, 88.148

◄ 125

The Cloud, 1908
Alvin L. Coburn, English (born
   American) (1882-1966)
Photogravure
H: 14 3/8" (365 mm)
W: 10 1/2" (267 mm)
The Spencer Museum of Art;
   anonymous gift, 83.75

126 ➤

The Ferry, 1910
Alvin L. Coburn, English (born
    American) (1822-1966)
Photogravure
H: 5 3/8" (138 mm)
W: 7" (177 mm)
The Spencer Museum of Art;
    anonymous gift, 83.78

◄ **127**

Untitled, ca. 1900
Gertrude Käsebier, American
    (1852–1934)
Gum bichromate print
H: 5 3/8" (138 mm)
W: 7 1/4" (185 mm)
The Spencer Museum of Art; gift of
    Mrs. Hermine M. Turner, 73.31

◄ **128**

Untitled, ca. 1900
Gertrude Käsebier, American
    (1852–1934)
Gum bichromate print
H: 7 5/8" (193 mm)
W: 5 7/8" (149 mm)
The Spencer Museum of Art; gift of
    Mrs. Hermine M. Turner, 73.18

BIBLIOGRAPHY

Achilles

Achilles, Rolf. *"The Chap-Book* and Posters of Stone & Kimball at The Newberry Library." *The Journal of Decorative and Propaganda Arts* (Fall 1989); 64-77.

Adams

Adams, Steven. *The Arts and Crafts Movement.* Seacaucus, N.J.: Chartwell Books, 1987.

Anscombe and Gere

Anscombe, Isabelle, and Charlotte Gere. *Arts and Crafts in Britain and America.* New York: Rizzoli, 1978.

Apostol

Apostol, Jane. *Will Bradley.* Pasadena, Cal.: The Weather Bird Press, 1976.

Aslin

Aslin, Elizabeth. *Nineteenth Century English Furniture.* London: Faber and Faber, 1962.

———. *The Aesthetic Movement: Prelude to Art Nouveau.* New York: Excalibur Books, 1969.

Atterbury and Batkin

Atterbury, Paul, and Maureen Batkin. *The Dictionary of Minton.* Woodbridge, England: Antique Collectors' Club, 1990.

Banham and Harris

Banham, Joanna, and Jennifer Harris, eds. *William Morris and the Middle Ages* (exhibition catalogue). Whitworth Art Gallery, Manchester, England: University Press, 1984.

Bavaro and Mossman

Bavaro, Joseph, and Thomas Mossman. *The Furniture of Gustav Stickley.* New York: Van Nostrand Reinhold, 1982.

Berman

Berman, Avis. "Antiques: Liberty Siver." *Architectural Digest* 47, no. 2 (February 1990): 188–93.

Blasberg

Blasberg, Robert. *Fulper Art Pottery: An Aesthetic Appreciation 1909–1929* (exhibition catalogue). New York: The Jordan-Volpe Gallery, 1979.

Breitenbach

Breitenbach, Edgar. "The Poster Craze." *American Heritage* 13, no. 2 (February 1962): 26–31.

Brown University
William Morris and the Kelmscott Press (exhibition catalogue). Providence, R.I.: Brown University, 1960.

Bruhn
Bruhn, Thomas. *American Decorative Tiles 1870–1930* (exhibition catalogue). The William Benton Museum of Art, Storrs, Conn.: The University of Connecticut, 1979.

Bumpus
Bumpus, Bernard. "Frederick Hurten Rhead: A Natural Offshoot of His Family." *Arts & Crafts Quarterly* 3, no. 3 (1990): 4–9.

Carpenter
Carpenter, Charles. *Gorham Silver 1831–1981.* New York: Dodd, Mead & Co., 1982.

Cathers
Cathers, David, ed. *Stickley Craftsman Furniture Catalogues: Unabridged Reprints of Two Mission Furniture Catalogs.* New York: Dover Publications, 1979.

———. *Furniture of the American Arts and Crafts Movement.* New York: New American Library, 1981.

Cincinnati Historical Society
2,292 Pieces of Early Rookwood in the Cincinnati Art Museum in 1916. Reprint, Cincinnati: Cincinnati Historical Society, 1978.

Cirker
Cirker, Hayward, and Blanche Cirker, eds. *The Golden Age of the Poster.* New York: Dover Publications, 1971.

Clark and Hughto
Clark, Garth, and Margie Hughto. *A Century of Ceramics in the United States 1878–1916* (exhibition catalogue). New York: Everson Museum of Art, 1979.

Clark, Ellison, and Hecht
Clark, Garth, Robert Ellison, Jr., and Eugene Hecht. *The Mad Potter of Biloxi: The Art and Life of George E. Ohr.* New York: Abbeville, 1989.

Clark
Clark, Robert Judson, ed. *The Arts and Crafts Movement in America 1876–1916* (exhibition catalogue). Princeton, N.J.: Princeton University Art Museum, 1972.

———, ed. "Aspects of the Arts and Crafts Movement in America." *Record of the Princeton University Art Museum* 34, no. 2 (1975).

Cooper-Hewitt Museum
American Art Pottery. New York: Cooper-Hewitt Museum, 1987.

Coysh
Coysh, Arthur Wilfred. *British Art Pottery 1870–1940.* Rutland, Vt.: Tuttle & Co., 1976.

Dale

Dale, Sharon. *Frederick Hurten Rhead: An English Potter in America* (exhibition catalogue). Erie, Penn.: Erie Art Museum, 1986.

Darling

Darling, Sharon. *Chicago Metalsmiths* (exhibition catalogue). Chicago: Chicago Historical Society, 1977.

_____. *Chicago Ceramics and Glass: An Illustrated History from 1871 to 1933* (exhibition catalogue). Chicago: Chicago Historical Society, 1979.

_____. *Teco: Art Pottery of the Prairie School* (exhibition catalogue). Erie, Penn.: Erie Art Museum, 1989.

Dempsey

Dempsey, Bruce. *Beauty Fixed in Many Mediums* (exhibition catalogue). Talahassee, Fla.: Florida State University, 1972.

Dietz

Dietz, Ulysses. *The Newark Museum Collection of American Art Pottery.* Newark, N.J.: Newark Museum, 1984.

DiNoto

DiNoto, Andrea. "A Certain Shade of Green: The Happy Collaboration Between Two Collectors and an Art Dealer." *Conoisseur*, 215 no. 883 (August 1985): 50–57.

Donhauser

Donhauser, Paul. *History of American Ceramics: The Studio Potter.* Dubuque, Iowa: Kendall/Hunt Publishing Co., 1978.

Doros

Doros, Paul. *The Tiffany Collection of the Chrysler Museum at Norfolk* (exhibition catalogue). Norfolk, Va.: Norfolk Museum, 1978.

Duncan

Duncan, Alastair. *Tiffany at Auction.* New York: Rizzoli, 1981.

Duncan, Eidelberg, and Harris

Duncan, Alastair, Martin Eidelberg, and Neil Harris. *Masterworks of Louis Comfort Tiffany.* New York: Abrams, 1989.

Eidelberg

Eidelberg, Martin. "The Ceramic Art of William H. Grueby." *Conoisseur* 184, no. 739 (September 1973): 47–54.

_____, ed. *From Our Native Clay: Art Pottery from the Collections of the American Ceramic Arts Society* (exhibition catalogue). New York: American Ceramic Arts Society, 1987.

Evans

Evans, Paul. *Art Pottery of the United States.* 2d edition. New York: Feingold and Lewis, 1987.

Eyles

Eyles, Desmond. *The Doulton Burslem Wares.* London: Barrie & Jenkins, 1980.

Garner
Garner, Philippe, ed. *The Encyclopedia of Decorative Arts 1890–1940.* New York: Chartwell Books, 1978.

Gengarelly and Derby
Gengarelly, W. Anthony, and Carol Derby. *The Prendergasts and the Arts and Crafts Movement* (exhibition catalogue). Williamstown, Australia: Williams College Museum of Art, 1989.

Gibson
Gibson, David. *Designed to Persuade: The Graphic Art of Edward Penfield* (exhibition catalogue). Yonkers, N.Y.: The Hudson River Museum of Westchester, 1984.

Gloag
Gloag, John. *The Englishman's Chair.* London: Allen & Unwin, 1964.

Goddu
Goddu, Joseph. *American Art Posters of the 1890s* (exhibition catalogue). New York: Hirschl & Adler, 1989.

Gray and Edwards
Gray, Stephen, and Robert Edwards, eds. *Collected Works of Gustav Stickley.* Reprint, New York: Turn of the Century Editions, 1981.

Gray
Gray, Stephen, ed. *Arts and Crafts Furniture: Shop of the Crafters at Cincinnati.* New York: Turn of the Century Editions, 1983.

_____, ed. *A Catalogue of the Roycrofters.* New York: Turn of the Century Editions, 1989.

Hanks and Peirce
Hanks, David, and Donald Peirce. *The Virginia Carroll Crawford Collection of American Decorative Arts, 1825–1917.* Atlanta: High Museum of Art, 1983.

Harvard University
The Turn of the Century 1885–1910 (exhibition catalogue). The Houghton Library, Cambridge, Mass.: Harvard University, 1970.

Haslam
Haslam, Malcolm. *English Art Pottery, 1865–1915.* Woodbridge, England: Antique Collectors' Club, 1975.

_____. *Collector's Style Guide: Arts and Crafts.* New York: Ballantine Books, 1988.

Henzke
Henzke, Lucile. *Art Pottery of America.* Exton, Penn.: Schiffer Pub., 1982.

Hillier
Hillier, Bevis. *Posters.* London: Spring Books, 1974.

Hills
Hills, Patricia. *Turn of the Century America* (exhibition catalogue). New York: Whitney Museum of Art, 1977.

Hirschl & Adler

From Architecture to Object: Masterworks of the Arts and Crafts Movement (exhibition catalogue). New York: Hirschl & Adler, 1989.

Hornung

Hornung, Clarence, ed. *Will Bradley: His Graphic Art.* New York: Dover Publications, 1974.

Hyland and Stokstad

Hyland, Douglas, and Marilyn Stokstad, eds. *Catalogue of the Sculpture Collection.* Lawrence, Kan.: Spencer Museum of Art, 1981.

Hyman

Hyman, Helen. *Design to Persuade: American Literary Advertising Posters of the 1890s* (exhibition catalogue). New Haven, Conn.: Yale University Art Gallery, 1978.

Johnson

Johnson, Diane C. "Art Nouveau in America: Three Posters by Will H. Bradley." *The Register of the Museum of Art* (Spencer Museum of Art, University of Kansas) 4, nos. 4–5 (1971): 62–77.

_____. *American Art Nouveau.* New York: Abrams, 1979.

Kaplan

Kaplan, Wendy, ed. *"The Art That is Life": The Arts and Crafts Movement in America, 1875–1920* (exhibition catalogue). Boston: Museum of Fine Arts, 1987.

_____, ed. *The Encyclopedia of Arts and Crafts: The International Movement, 1850–1920.* New York: E. P. Dutton, 1989.

Keay

Keay, Carolyn. *American Posters of the Turn of the Century.* London: Academy Editions, 1975.

Keen

Keen, Kirsten. *American Art Pottery 1875–1930* (exhibition catalogue). Wilmington, Del.: Delaware Art Museum, 1978.

Kiehl

Kiehl, David. *American Art Posters of the 1890s in the Metropolitan Museum of Art.* New York: The Metropolitan Museum of Art, 1987.

Koch

Koch, Robert. *Louis Comfort Tiffany* (exhibition catalogue). New York: Museum of Contemporary Crafts of the American Craftsmen's Council, 1958.

_____. "Artistic Books, Periodicals and Posters of the 'Gay Nineties'." *The Art Quarterly* 25, no. 4 (Winter 1962): 371–83.

_____. *Louis C. Tiffany, Rebel in Glass.* New York: Crown Publishers, 1964.

_____. "The Pottery of Artus Van Briggle." *Art In America* 52, no. 3 (June 1964): 120–22.

_____. "Elbert Hubbard's Roycrofters as Artist-Craftsmen." *Winterthur Portfolio* 3 (1967): 67–82.

_____. *Louis C. Tiffany's Glass, Bronzes, Lamps.* New York: Crown Publishers, 1971; reprint 1989.

_____. *Louis C. Tiffany's Art Glass.* New York, Crown Publishers, 1977.

Kovel
Kovel, Ralph, and Terry Kovel. *The Kovels' Collector's Guide to American Art Pottery.* New York: Crown Publishers, 1974.

Kurland-Zabar
Reflections: Arts and Crafts Metalwork in England and the United States (exhibition catalogue). New York: Kurland-Zabar, 1990.

Lambourne
Lambourne, Lionel. *Utopian Craftsmen: The Arts and Crafts Movement from the Cotswolds to Chicago.* Salt Lake City, Utah: Peregrine Smith, 1980.

Levy
Levy, Mervyn. *Liberty Style: The Classic Years, 1898–1910.* New York: Rizzoli, 1986.

Ludwig
Ludwig, Coy. *The Arts and Crafts Movement in New York State, 1890s–1920s* (exhibition catalogue). New York: Hamilton, 1983.

Loring
Loring, John. "American Art Pottery." *Conoisseur* 200, no. 806 (April 1979): 279–85.

Malhotra, Thom, et. al.
Malhotra, Ruth, Christina Thom, et. al. *Das fruhe Plakat in Europa und den USA.* 2 vols. Berlin: Gebr. Mann Verlag, 1973.

Margolin
Margolin, Victor. *American Poster Renaissance.* New York: Watson-Guptill Publications, 1975.

McKean
McKean, Hugh. *The "Lost" Treasures of Louis Comfort Tiffany.* New York: Doubleday & Co., 1980.

_____. *The Treasures of Tiffany* (exhibition catalogue). Chicago: Museum of Science and Industry, 1982.

McKenna
McKenna, Paul. *A History and Bibliography of the Roycroft Printing Shop.* North Tonawada, N.Y.: Tona Graphics, 1986.

Metropolitan Museum of Art
Nineteenth-Century America: Furniture and Other Decorative Arts. New York: Metropolitan Museum of Art, 1970.

Moffatt

Moffatt, Frederick. *Arthur Wesley Dow.* Washington, D.C.: Smithsonian Institution Press, 1977.

Mollman

Mollman, Sarah. *Louis Sullivan in the Art Institute of Chicago: The Illustrated Catalogue of Collections.* New York: Garland Pub., 1989.

Morris

Morris, Barbara. *Liberty Design 1874–1914.* London: Chartwell Books, Inc., 1989.

Naylor

Naylor, Gillian. *The Arts and Crafts Movement.* London: Trefoil Publications, 1971.

Nelson

Nelson, Marion J. "Art Nouveau in American Ceramics." *The Art Quarterly* 26 (1963): 441–59.

_____. *Art Pottery in the Midwest* (exhibition catalogue). Minneapolis: University of Minnesota Art Museum, 1988.

Nylander, Redmond, and Sander

Nylander, Richard, Elizabeth Redmond, and Penny Sander. *Wallpaper in New England* (exhibition catalogue). Boston: Society for the Preservation of New England Antiquities, 1986.

Oman and Hamilton

Oman, Charles, and Jean Hamilton. *Wallpapers: An International History and Illustrated Survey from the Victoria and Albert Museum.* New York: Abrams, 1982.

Ormond and Irvine

Ormond, Suzanne, and Mary Irvine. *Louisiana's Art Nouveau: The Crafts of the Newcomb Style.* New York: Pelican Publishing Co., 1976.

Peck

Peck, Herbert. *The Book of Rookwood Pottery.* New York: Crown Publishers, 1968.

Préaud and Gauthier

Préaud, Tamara, and Serge Gauthier. *Ceramics of the Twentieth Century.* New York: Rizzoli, 1982.

Taylor

Taylor, John Russell. *The Art Nouveau Book in Britain.* London: Methuen & Co., Ltd., 1966.

Thompson, P.

Thompson, Paul. *The Work of William Morris.* London: Quartet Books, 1977.

Thompson, S. O.

Thompson, Susan Otis. *American Book Design and William Morris.* New York and London: R. R. Bowker Company, 1977.

Tilbrook

Tilbrook, Adrian J. *The Designs of Archibald Knox for Liberty & Co.* London: Ornament Press, 1976.

Toledo Museum of Art
The Art of Louis Comfort Tiffany (exhibition catalogue). Toledo, Ohio: The Toledo Museum of Art, 1978.

Topeka Public Library
Rookwood Pottery: A Centennial Celebration, 1880–1980 (exhibition catalogue). Topeka, Kan.: Topeka Public Library Gallery of Fine Arts, 1980.

Trapp
Trapp, Kenneth. *Ode to Nature: Flowers and Landscapes of the Rookwood Pottery 1880–1940* (exhibition catalogue). New York: Jordan-Volpe Gallery, 1980.

_____. *Toward the Modern Style: Rookwood Pottery, the Later Years, 1915–50* (exhibition catalogue). New York: Jordan-Volpe Gallery, 1983.

_____. "Rediscovering the Arts and Crafts Movement." *Antiques and Fine Art* 7, no. 3 (March/April 1990): 85–91.

Victoria and Albert Museum
Liberty's 1875–1975 (exhibition catalogue). London: Victoria and Albert Museum, 1975.

Volpe and Cathers
Volpe, Todd, and Beth Cathers. *Treasures of the American Arts and Crafts Movement, 1890–1920.* New York: Abrams, 1988.

Ward
Ward, Roger, ed. *A Bountiful Decade: Selected Acquisitions 1977–1987* (exhibition catalogue). Kansas City, Mo.: Nelson-Atkins Museum of Art, 1987.

Watkinson
Watkinson, Raymond. *William Morris as Designer.* New York: Reinhold Pub., 1967.

Wong
Wong, Roberta Waddell. *Bradley: American Artist and Craftsman* (exhibition catalogue). New York: The Metropolitan Museum of Art, 1972.

Wooden
Wooden, Howard. *Art of a Changing Society: British Watercolors and Drawings 1775–1900* (exhibition catalogue). Wichita, Kan.: Wichita Art Museum, 1983.

INDEX